Moral Economy and American Realistic Novels

Modern American Literature

Yoshinobu Hakutani
General Editor

Vol. 2

PETER LANG
New York • Washington, D.C./Baltimore
Bern • Frankfurt am Main • Berlin • Vienna • Paris

Da Zheng

Moral Economy and American Realistic Novels

PETER LANG
New York • Washington, D.C./Baltimore
Bern • Frankfurt am Main • Berlin • Vienna • Paris

Library of Congress Cataloging-in-Publication Data

Zheng, Da.
Moral economy and American realistic novels/ Da Zheng.
p. cm. — (Modern American literature; vol. 2)
Includes bibliographical references (p.) and index.
1. American fiction—19th century—History and criticism—
Theory, etc. 2. Realism in literature. 3. Economics—Moral and ethical
aspects. 4. Moral conditions in literature. 5. Economics in literature. 6. Ethics
in literature. 7. Narration (Rhetoric). 8. Twain, Mark, 1835–1910. Gilded
age. 9. Howells, William Dean, 1837–1920. Hazard of new fortunes.
10. Fuller, Henry Blake, 1857–1929. Cliff-dwellers. 11. Fuller, Henry Blake,
1857–1929. With the procession. I. Title. II. Series: Modern American
literature (New York, N.Y.); vol. 2.
PS374.R37Z48 813'.40912—dc20 94-49414
ISBN 0-8204-2773-X
ISSN 1078-0521

Die Deutsche Bibliothek-CIP-Einheitsaufnahme

Zheng, Da:
Moral economy and American realistic novels/Da Zheng.
–New York; Washington, D.C./Baltimore; Bern; Frankfurt am Main; Berlin;
Vienna; Paris: Lang.
(Modern American literature; Vol. 2)
ISBN 0-8204-2773-X
NE: G

Cover design by James F. Brisson.

The paper in this book meets the guidelines for permanence and durability
of the Committee on Production Guidelines for Book Longevity
of the Council of Library Resources.

Printed in the United States of America.

To my parents
with love and gratitude

Acknowledgments

An earlier version of Chapter I has been published in the *CLA Journal*, and I gratefully acknowledge permission to use the material.

I want to thank my former teachers and friends at Boston University and my colleagues at Suffolk University for their interest in my work. Their constructive suggestions have helped me to refine this work, and I would like to take this opportunity to express my deep appreciation and gratitude.

I also want to thank Professor William L. Vance of Boston University for his shrewd criticism and acute directions at every stage of this project. His inexhaustible patience, humane understanding, and exceptional expertise have left their marks on this final product as well as its numerous drafts. From him, I have learned a great deal. I have, above all, apprehended the meaning, the need, and the importance of a mentor.

Finally, I want to thank my son, Leon, for his curiosity and pride in my work, and my wife, Min Yang, for her unwavering support and enthusiastic encouragement.

Contents

Introduction

In the *New York Tribune* of September 27, 1871, Mark Twain published "The Revised Catechism," in which he underlined the fact that money had become the dominant standard of the country.

> Q: What is the chief end of man?
> A: To get rich.
> Q: In what way?
> A: Dishonestly if we can, honestly if we must.
> Q: Who is God, the only one and true?
> A: Money is God. Gold and greenbacks and stocks—father, son and the ghost of the same—three persons in one. . . .
> Q: Who were the models the young were taught to emulate in former days?
> A: Washington and Franklin.
> Q: Whom do they and should they emulate now in this era of enlightenment?
> A: Tweed, Hall, Connelly, Camochan, Fisk, Gould, Barnard, and Winans.[1]

What Mark Twain wrote was really a biting yet precise comment on the Gilded Age from 1865 to 1890. Indeed, as William Dean Howells commented through Bromfield Corey in *The Rise of Silas Lapham,* money had come "to the fore now. It is romance, the poetry of our age."[2] The year of 1865 marked both the end of the Civil War and the beginning of the age of money. The national market economy replaced the mercantile economy, and the great transformation began which led to the corporate economy by the end of the century. With railroad construction, urbanization, territorial expansion, and many other events, the nation was booming on a heretofore unimaginable scale.[3]

It goes without saying that socioeconomic facts in the Gilded Age became materials for the writers of the time. Many novels published at the time showed a general interest in the contemporary socioeconomic activities. Speculation, fierce competition, and pursuit of fashion—three major traits of the Gilded Age America—became subjects in the depiction of this fascinating period in many realistic novels. Mark Twain, for example, underlined (in)sanity in his metaphorical presentation of the widespread speculation. William Dean Howells showed an ethical concern for the aftermath of fierce competition with a stress on the issue of sympathy. Henry Blake Fuller, a Chicago writer, caught the topic of attention-seeking in his response to social fashions.

Truly, the relation of the realistic novels to the socioeconomic system has been much studied, but without observing how novelists presented and responded to these major traits. Claude Reherd Flory's *Economic Criticism in American Fiction: 1792-1900* (1936) and Walter F. Taylor's *The Economic Novel in America* (1942) represent pioneering efforts in exploring the prominent feature of economics in American novels. Flory's book, which studies about 250 novels of the period from 1792 to 1900, claims that these novels, with a general concern with economics, present the novelists' critical responses to the social, political, and economic problems. Taylor's book, with a sharp focus on five major American novelists of the late nineteenth century, among whom are Mark Twain and William Dean Howells, gives an excellent discussion of the economic background against which these "economic novels" were produced.[4] Nevertheless, the subtlety and complexity of the novelists' attitudes toward the economy as shown in the realistic texts are often overlooked or superficially treated. Flory, for example, states that the capitalists' "subtle and insidious control" of the government "receives wide condemnation in the pages of our critical economic fiction."[5] He fails to perceive, however, that the interest of these novelists did not always lead to a condemnation of the capital and the capitalists' control of the government. Instead, their treatment of these subjects was often reserved and ambivalent. Moreover, Flory has neglected the wide range of interest of these economic novels in speculation, competition, fashion, and exchange, factors that changed human relationships and exerted no less power on society than what capitalists did with the government.

The Image of Money (1969), by Jan W. Dietrichson, gives a thorough discussion of the image and function of money in Henry James and Howells. However, the book leaves untouched some important economic issues which may not have money directly involved: an invitation to a dinner, a new name or title gained, or even an advance in social status.

These are economic issues because they all involve exchange and human relations and may be seen as special forms of economic activity. Dietrichson's book was written at the time when historians were re-viewing the past scholarly discoveries. For example, Matthew Josephson's loaded coinage "Robber Barons," referring to the business leaders of the Gilded Age, was challenged by the new theory that stressed these entrepreneurs' indispensable contribution to the economic growth in the United States.[6] Dietrichson, in his historical examination of money, unveils the critical views of the novelists about wealth and the Gilded Age, and he also underlines their recognition and appreciation of the essential and liberating power that money could exercise.[7]

The late seventies and eighties saw a breakthrough in the study of the economic aspect of American novels. Marc Shell proposes the theory of "economy of literature" in his two important books, *The Economy of Literature* (1978) and *Money, Language and Thought* (1982).[8] Shell points out that similarities exist between metaphorization (in language and literature) and economic representation and exchange. The economy of literature seeks to study the relation between literary exchanges and the economic exchange.[9]

> This participation of economic form in literature and philosophy, even in the discourse about truth, is defined neither by what literature and philosophy talk about (sometimes money, sometimes not) nor by why they talk about it (sometimes for money, sometimes not) but rather by the tropic interaction between economic and linguistic symbolization and production. A formal money of the mind informs all discourse and is as unaffected by whether or not the thematic content of a particular work includes money as by whether or not the material content of the ink in which the work may be inscribed includes gold.[10]

Shell brings us a fresh view of literature. His theory extends the scope of the accepted concept of economy, and it propounds that all literary works can be studied in terms of "economic form," though only some of them can be analyzed in terms of "economic content."[11] Besides, Shell's theory also redefines the role of the writer as an economist who conducts arrangement of characters and plots for the best effect in his creative writing activity.

Similarly, Michael T. Gilmore, Walter Benn Michaels, Wai-Chee Dimock, as well as a number of other critics no longer limit their study to the literal description of money or economic activities in the text. These critics seek to understand the relation between literary exchange (e.g., metaphors, structures, and language) and the exchanges in the external social context. The literary exchange is shown to be shaped by the external political and economic exchanges, yet literature is also to reflect, interfere with, and mediate these exchanges. Gilmore, for example, regards literary products as commodities, and literary creation as analogous to industrial production. In *American Romanticism and the Marketplace* (1985), Gilmore demonstrates the influence of the marketplace on American romanticism and analyzes the complex relationship between writers and the marketplace as shown in their ambivalent responses to the socioeconomic changes in the first half of the nineteenth century. Gilmore argues that the "two developments, the commercialization of society and of culture, profoundly affected the American romantics and had a shaping influence on the themes and form of their art."[12]

Michaels's *The Gold Standard and the Logic of Naturalism* (1987) is a New Historicist reconsideration of some of the fiction produced between mid-nineteenth century and the turn of the century.[13] Michaels accepts the belief that literary works should be studied in relation to the economic conditions and the cultural values in which they appeared. Michaels's stance differs from that of traditional literary historians, such as Walter F. Taylor, in at least two ways: one, Michaels perceives all social activities as essentially economic since they involve evaluation, exchange, or agreement; two, Michaels locates in the fictional text an allusion to the contemporary economic issue (such as the gold standard in *McTeague*, or the corporation in *The Octopus*), and examines the issue to show that the text was socially and economically engaged. Dimock makes a similar approach in her study of Edith Wharton's *The House of Mirth* and William Dean Howells's *The Rise of Silas Lapham*, with focuses on exchange and pain, respectively.[14] Dimock stresses the "direct link" between "the formal arrangement inside the novel" and "the social engagements outside a novel." She uses the term "formal referentiality" to specify the relation between the novel form as "a system of distribution and adequation," and the economic system outside fiction.[15]

The aim of my book is to further the study that recent critics, particularly Michaels and Dimock, have begun, with a specific focus on the realistic novelists' presentation of and response to the major traits of the Gilded Age. Four works will be examined: *The Gilded Age* (1873) by Mark Twain and Charles Dudley Warner, *A Hazard of New Fortunes* (1890) by William Dean Howells, and *Cliff-Dwellers* (1893) and *With the Procession* (1895) by Henry Blake Fuller. The rationale behind the choice of these texts is two-fold: one, these are major works by major realistic writers of the period and, except *A Hazard of New Fortunes*, they have not received enough of the critical attention which they deserve; two, each of these novels clearly demonstrates its interest in one of the three major aspects of the time—speculation, competition, and the pursuit of fashions. And each responds to the socioeconomic reality in a distinctive way. Taken together, these novels provide a broad view of these realistic writers' fictional engagement with the period as well as a new dimension of realism.

Economic Content

Realistic novels are never literally realistic in their reflection of the socioeconomic reality. As cultural products, they merely offer systems of signs, referring to the signified. The meaning of these signs is referential but slippery, inviting infinite interpretation, and there is never a definitive correspondence between the sign and the signified. Further, during the process of producing these signs, novelists select, arrange, and omit details. They are subjectively involved in the literary creation of a reality in literature.

Yet, realistic novels, colored by the subjective interference of the writer, are realistic precisely because of those signs and selected, arranged, and suppressed details. A novel with such artistic selection can actually be a more accurate picture of reality than a mechanically faithful presentation. The details per se, selected or hidden, are important; yet more important is the motif of the period revealed through these details. The term "motif" refers to the salient tone, issue, or image that recurs throughout the novel and that is often closely related to one of the major traits of the period. The details are numbered, limited, and local; the motif, however, is essential, representative, and comprehensive. For this reason, highlighting the motifs in American realistic novels and examining the ways that novelists presented these motifs can be the key to a sound grasp of realistic novels.

It is equally important to examine these realistic novels together with some of the non-fiction of the time. Writings are cultural products, and they are never truly autonomous though they often appear to be. These novels seem to be very different from the non-fiction writing, but they are actually homogeneous in nature since they all share and reflect the motifs of the period. Placing a text in its historical context by examining other contemporary non-fiction, may help one apprehend a motif in society and consequently detect and understand the motif in the literary text.

The Gilded Age, the novel that gives the name to the period, conveys an outstanding trait of the time: feverish money-making and speculation.[16] This feature might be defined as neither sane nor insane, for it was really both insane and sane. The capitalist economy, with abundant opportunities for speculation and systematic management in its operation, often appears highly rational and scientific; yet a strain of irrationality—as seen in the illusions and delusions that usually accompany speculation—coexists with this characteristic of sanity in the core of the system. The feature of (in)sanity is the very motif of *The Gilded Age*. The novel provides a favorable condition to the dream of the Hawkinses who aspire to become rich through land speculation and, at various stages of the novel, the family dream seems on the brink of becoming true.

The title of the novel, a wonderful analogy, pinpoints the fact that it is a period of exciting confusion. The age, being gilded, is neither gold nor non-gold, since it is both gold and non-gold. This very issue is best represented by the famous issue of paper money in post-bellum America. Thomas Nast's drawing "Milk-Tickets for Babies, In Place of Milk" for *Robinson Crusoe's Money*, illustrates the mixture of representation and reality, absurdity, and reason in the paper money issue. In the drawing, Nast juxtaposes several pieces of paper: one made into a house, one into a cow, and still another into money, by acts of an "architect," an "artist," and congress, respectively.[17] The line that differentiates the "real" from something that simply "represents" gets blurred, and everyone can act as an alchemist. Frank Norris's *McTeague* (1899), in this sense, accurately captures the same motif of its time. If paper could become money and a sign could become what it signifies through the art of designation, McTeague's love of the gold tooth and Zerkow's passion for collecting junk are nothing but rational. And it seems not totally absurd for an infatuated Zerkow to believe obstinately in the existence of the gold plates fabricated by Maria's narratives.[18]

Twain's works are full of such cases of fervent trust in forged or false facts, and a firm belief in, or (mis)reading of, sham: "granite rubbish and nasty glittering mica" on the ground are perceived as silver in *Roughing It* (1872); a well-dressed pauper is welcomed and hailed as Prince in *The Prince and the Pauper* (1882); a poor city vagrant with a million-pound note is recognized and respected as a millionaire in *The £1,000,000 Banknote* (1893); a black slave and his master exchange their positions and identity without their own awareness in *Puddn'head Wilson* (1894). Through a series of such instances, Twain shows that the nation suffered from blindness, a wide-spread social epidemic caused by the glittering pieces of "gold."

Howells takes the city of New York as the setting for *A Hazard of New Fortunes*. The novel, through the Marches' house-hunting tour in the city, draws a map of chaos, class division, and economic inequality as well as the geographical physicality. Howells's interest is to underline the cause—lack of sympathy—of all these social problems. Howells expresses the criticism:

> The whole at moments seemed to him [March] lawless, Godless; the absence of intelligent, comprehensive purpose in the huge disorder, and the violent struggle to subordinate the result to the greater good, penetrated with its dumb appeal the consciousness of a man who had always been too self-enwrapt to perceive the chaos to which *the individual selfishness* must always lead.[19] [emphasis mine]

The individual selfishness, or lack of sympathy, leads to material prosperity, but it also widens the gap between the wealthy and the poor.[20] "Progress and poverty," a juxtaposition of two seemingly unrelated terms that Henry George uses for the title of his famous book in 1880, challenges the concept "progress" as often employed to define American economic development and material prosperity. George maintains that wherever there are conditions favorable to material development, there concurs "the deepest poverty, the sharpest struggle for existence, and the most enforced idleness."[21] Jacob Riis's famous account of the living conditions of the working class people in New York tenements in *How The*

Other Half Lives reinforces Henry George's observation. Immigrants in the new industrial era, uprooted and wretched, suffer from epidemics, improper nourishment, and many other harsh living conditions. The capitalist system is condemned as "a slavery as real as any that ever disgraced the South."[22] In Howells's utopian novel, *A Traveller from Altruria* (1894), the novelist comments through Homos, a detached observer, that Labor is at war with Capital in America, and both the rich and the poor are slaves of greed. He suggests that only human affection and good-will can possibly cross the class line to mitigate this warfare.[23]

What George and Riis, as well as Howells, have achieved is more than presenting a blunt inversion of the material prospect ideal. They drew the attention of the public to the social and cultural isolation resulting from class division that never before occurred in American history. Sympathy, or brotherly feelings, became a rare commodity in the national market economy. And these writers, with their "unvarnished" view, as Jean-Christopher Agnew has commented on Riis's work, "effectively mimicked the voyeurism of the society columns" by presenting "candid" snapshots of those areas inaccessible to or neglected by other parts of the society.[24] These writers presented the labor that had been neglected by a society interested in competition and achievement in the popular success stories. They also presented to the public those areas shadowed by the skyscrapers, hidden by the L, and silenced by the powerful voice of money.

Henry Blake Fuller's two novels, which were published only a few years after Howells's novel, present another important motif of the society: attention-seeking. From the 1880s to the end of the nineteenth century occurred the great merger movement when more and more middle-sized enterprises were integrated vertically and horizontally to form large corporations. These new corporations operated their own nation-wide marketing systems and had a direct control of raw materials and production.[25] With the great merger movement, accompanied by the completion of the railroad construction, the construction of skyscrapers, and the growth of the national and urban market, there appeared tycoons such as William Rockefeller, Andrew Carnegie, James Fisk, Henry Clay Frick, Jay Gould, and the DuPonts, who controlled the national economy and industry and attracted much attention from the society.

To the general public, a painful realization of the loss of identity and the need to search for attention consequently followed. In this systematically organized society, the majority of the workers, who occupied various positions in the grid of the socioeconomic system, were merely playing mechanical business roles in the whole process of operation. The attention was mainly given to the few top tycoons and executives. Anxiety and anguish were the emotions that many people experienced when left in obscurity. Seeking attention and giving attention became an essential mode of interpersonal relations, and this was precisely what Thorstein Veblen, a profound social critic, was trying to demonstrate in *The Theory of the Leisure Class* (1899).[26] Popular self-help books, such as *Pushing to the Front* (1894) by Orison S. Marden, were advocating the will to emerge successful and outstanding with persistence and courage. Theodore Dreiser's *Sister Carrie* (1900), Frank Norris's *The Octopus* (1901), and Upton Sinclair's *The Jungle* (1906) offer some glimpses of the material culture of the time. Fuller's novels, in underlining this motif of attention-seeking, use two metaphors—a skyscraper and a procession—to stand for the collectivity in social and economic structures. The economic activities in these novels—sometimes dealing with money, and very often with no money involved—all strive to catch and win attention for the single purpose of surviving in the rigorous life of competition.

It should be noted that each of these three motifs—insanity, lack of sympathy, and attention-seeking—dictates a special form of "money" and involves some pecuniary functions, such as payment and circulation. In Fuller's novels, attention is being pursued for its power to advance or secure the pursuer's social position. Gaining money becomes less important than gaining attention since the latter promises a greater, sometimes an ever increasing, amount of profit in the form of social advancement as well as money. In Mark Twain's world of speculation, insanity circulates like money. It is sugar-coated, or rather alloyed, with sanity. For Howells's world, sympathy, rare and limited, is also a form of "money." Competition in modern industrial society has minimized the need of sympathy and limited the space for sympathy to circulate. In a sense, New York, infected with pneumonia and malaria, has been transformed into many isolated wards, among which there is hardly any communication or exchange of brotherly feelings. How to bring about an understanding among people and how to increase the circulation of sympathy in the city become critically important.

Form as Moral Critique

Ever since its emergence as a new genre, the novel has been carrying an ideological function of problem solving,[27] and much of this function is performed with its formal designs. By selecting, omitting, and arranging social facts, the novel exercises its explanatory and problem-solving capacities which no other cultural medium could adequately substitute for.

Contemporary critics, such as Eric Sundquist, Amy Kaplan, Philip Fisher and Walter Benn Michaels, have shown much interest in the complexities of the form of realism in relation to its ideological function. Both Sundquist and Kaplan argue that American realism as a genre was engaged with a society in flux, and it endeavored to construct a social world of conflict and change. Sundquist states that realists sought to "master a bewildering society that seemed always, in turn, to be mastering them" by returning to their imagination—"to its shaping and distorting powers."[28] To Kaplan, creative writing is essentially an act of "imagination and artistic management." Realistic writers never presented a picture without any subjective color. Confronted with the elusive process of social change, American realists, Kaplan argues, did not flee into imagination or nostalgia for a lost past; instead they presented a seemingly coherent social world they constructed.[29] Philip Fisher has made a similar assertion, though his reference extends to all the cultural work: "The ambition to redesign the common world is the ambition of the best instances of the cultural work." Romantic and realistic writers, James Fenimore Cooper, Harriet Beecher Stowe, and Theodore Dreiser, constructed the settlement, the Jeffersonian landscape, and the cities in their novels, and these "privileged settings," as Fisher argues, are meant to bring about a transformation of "whatever present appears unstructured, or, alternatively, fixed and representationally crowded."[30]

While agreeing that realistic novels carry out the role of social reconstruction through their formal designs, I would stress the economic interest of these novelists, and argue that a mark of subjective design in realistic novels is an imagined moral economy, a well-structured and stable world, opposed to the social reality. The moral economy is a utopian economic system devoid of chaos and disturbance. It is a bucolic country setting away from turmoil and fever of speculation, a unique literary enterprise where labor and capital become happily reconciled, or a shadowed theatre corner where the newly-wed couple could enjoy themselves without being observed by the attention-seeking crowd. These are the utopian spaces that novelists have created where social restrictions would not apply and economic turmoil would be reduced to mere shadow in the background.

The imagined moral economy reveals itself in the forms of these novels, especially in the conventionally unsatisfactory structural treatment. One example is the withdrawing or "failure" in the ending of these novels. The way these novels conclude deviates from those happy and rosy endings commonly seen in success stories by Horatio Alger or other popular writers. In *The Gilded Age*, Philip Sterling, as soon as he discovers the ore which he has been searching for months, suddenly gives up the mine; in *A Hazard of New Fortunes*, Dryfoos, who has been successful in his attempt to run a literary enterprise, unexpectedly transfers the magazine to Fulkerson and Basil March; and Burt Brainard, the son of a millionaire in *The Cliff-Dwellers*, ends up penniless. Another example can be seen in some seemingly unsatisfactory technical execution in these novels, such as the unbalanced, lengthy house-hunting scene in *A Hazard of New Fortunes*, or the digression in Laura Hawkins's trial scene in *The Gilded Age*.

Yet these "flaws" are on the very loci from which critical energy emanates. With these very "flaws," fever of speculation is cured, and the insane patient becomes sane; dissonance is silenced and sympathy will be abundant in circulation; conspicuous consumption is not appreciated and attention not pursued. In short, with these "flaws" and by creating utopian spaces, the novelists performed their criticism of the social reality. They did not mean to escape from such a reality; instead, they aimed for correction and remedy. The fact that the novel carries an ideological function is nowhere more obvious than here with these realistic novels, which invent some imaginary solutions to socioeconomic problems and contradictions, and decry the need for a moral reconstruction by contrasting these utopian solutions and a social reality.

The moral economy that these novels have designed reveals the ambivalent attitudes of these writers toward the economic system which they meant to rectify. As moral economists engaged in social critique, these realistic novelists were different from popular success-story writers, whose works, neatly structured and happily concluded, were apparently rosy but actually illusory.[31] Nevertheless, these realistic novelists, whose formal criticism was restrained and limited, were equally different from such radical critics as Henry George or Jacob Riis, whose criticism of the capitalist socioeconomic system was vehement and biting. The resolutions these novelists designed were utopian, and they did not really aim to destroy the present system. In fact, they all suggested a return to and dependence upon the system they were criticizing: Sellers will be a lawyer, Fulkerson and March continue the literary enterprise, and George Ogden and Abbie Brainard still situate themselves among the admirers of Ingles and contenders for attention. Realists, it may be thus said, often left a trace of appreciation and fascination in their criticism of the capitalist economy. There was often a tone of hope for a better future within that prevailing economy in their lament for failure or loss at the end. Moral economy is indeed a strategy of these realistic novelists to perform criticism without being convicted of lapse into either propaganda or escapism.

Chapter I

Economy of Insanity: *The Gilded Age*

One of the most memorable scenes in *The Gilded Age* is the trial of Laura Hawkins for the murder of Colonel Selby. Mr. Braham, Laura's defense attorney, after making his opening remarks, reminds the jury of its duty "to act officially," and pleads that it should "see that justice is done." Braham, trying to make an insanity defense for Laura, then proceeds to unfold "one of the most affecting dramas in all the history of misfortune."

> "I shall have to show you a life, the sport of fate and circumstances, hurried along through shifting storm and sun, bright with trusting innocence and anon black with heartless villainy, a career which moves on in love and desertion and anguish, always hovered over by the dark spectre of INSANITY,—an insanity hereditary and induced by mental torture,—until it ends, if end it must in your verdict, by one of those fearful accidents which are inscrutable to men and of which God alone knows the secret."[1]

Braham tells the court that Laura was born in a family "of wealth and refinement." The steamboat explosion on the Mississippi turned her into an orphan, her tender brain was severely stricken. This accident, nevertheless, is only "the prologue to the tragedy." During the Civil War, Selby, a Confederate officer, "plucked the sweetest bud" of this loveliest flower in the garden, "enjoyed its odor," and "trampled it in the mire beneath his feet." Years later, when Laura's family "have become enormously rich by . . . the discovery of immense mineral wealth" and when Laura is "engaged in a vast philanthropic scheme for the benefit of the poor," Selby comes back and attempts to force Laura to be "the mistress of his passion" again. Under such an intense situation when a spark could cause the explosion, Laura has no other choice but to commit this act. Though sensational and horrendous the murder has been, Laura, Braham argues, should be acquitted because she was not "in her right mind" at the moment when she committed the crime (499-50). Still, it was "the vengeance of Heaven," Braham insists. "Would the jury say that this retributive justice, inflicted by an outraged, a deluded woman, rendered irrational by the most cruel wrongs, was in the nature of a foul, premeditated murder?" (510-11).

Two sets of difficult questions have been posed here for the jury to contemplate in their deliberation. The first set is epistemological in nature: Was Laura truly insane when she committed murder? Can one ever determine Laura's true mental state at that particular moment? And how? And the second set is moral: Could this momentary insanity be an excuse for the defendant to escape from the legal liability? Or who is culpable if Laura could be excused? These difficult legal questions are simultaneously epistemological and moral in nature, as they are dealing with how to find truth and how to deal with abnormal behaviors. The process and the details of the jury's deliberation have been omitted in the novel, and we only hear their presumably unanimous verdict: "Not guilty." Yet, it is precisely this omission that has skipped over, or rather alerted us to, the point of controversy that has troubled the jury, the American public, and the authors Mark Twain and Charles Dudley Warner.

The insanity appeal and its subsequent knotty problems were neither fictional nor exceptional because they were heatedly discussed and debated in and outside the courtroom of the day. During the 1840s and 1850s, mental disease was on a steep rise in the United States, particularly in the northeast, at the highest rate in the world.[2] Psychiatrists then believed that the advance of civilization had harmed the human psyche by "complicating man's life and multiplying the demands made upon him."[3] Social and economic progress demanded and encouraged competition, which increased mental, emotional and psychical stress, and thus became detrimental to mental health.[4] The 1840 census results revealed the fact that a great proportion of the free black people were insane, and the only feasible explanation of this seemed to be the assumption that "freedom and a higher rate of civilization" were conducive to mental illness.[5] By presenting the trial of Laura Hawkins's horrendous murder case at the pivot of the novel, the authors successfully highlight insanity—a prominent feature of nineteenth-century American life—and the epistemological and moral questions that insanity entails. And the novel, with its realistic representation and form, reveals a concern with economic order and social stabilization as its response to a general socioeconomic phenomenon, which might be characterized as "insane."

In *The Oxford English Dictionary*, the first meaning of "insanity" is "the condition of being insane; unsoundness of mind as a consequence of brain-disease; madness, lunacy." The following are some of the major quotations cited by the Dictionary:

> a1677 Hale *Histo. Placit. Cor.* (R.). There is a partial insanity of mind and a total insanity. This partial insanity seems not to excuse them in the committing of any offence for its matter capital. 1722 *Junius Lett.* lxviii.355 Did they attempt to produce any evidence of his insanity? 1782 T. ARNOLD (*title*) Observations on the Nature, Kinds, Causes and Prevention of Insanity. 1827 SCOTT *Highl. Widow* v, The murder of an officer may be . . . coloured over with [the plea] of temporary insanity. 1859 *Engineer* VII. 282/2 Two cases of suicide . . . In each case the coroner's jury brought in a verdict of temporary insanity. 1865 *Pall Mall G.* 3 Aug. 4/1 The definition of insanity . . . as an inability to reason upon the evidence of the senses.[6]

These quotes provide a brief yet extremely interesting historical picture of the development in understanding insanity from an unsympathetic attitude toward a more lenient one. The nineteenth-century quotes, particularly the first one, evidence the emergence of the insanity plea and a different view of insanity.

Indeed, in the late eighteenth and early nineteenth centuries, there came a revolutionary change in the area of mental disease in both theory and practice in Europe. In 1792, Jean Baptiste Pinel in France and William Turke in England by pure coincidence simultaneously began to discard the theological doctrine of "possession" (especially the notion that insanity results from some spiritual influence), promote a scientific understanding of the nature of insanity, reform lunatic asylums, and treat the mental patients with "kindness and gentleness" rather than with "brutality and cruelty." The two reformers helped to win, in Andrew Dickson White's words, "one of the greatest, though one of the least known, triumphs of modern science and humanity."[7]

The early nineteenth century saw the emergence of the new science of psychiatry which brought about a fresh understanding of psychic mechanisms and thus challenged the traditional view of the "sane mind":

> Mental disorders came in different degrees and distinct varieties, and changed over time. The sane mind was not a pure intellect whose ability to "know," "think," and "understand" might be placed higher or lower along a linear scale of cognitive development, but rather a conglomerate of reason and emotion, a complex structure in which disturbances of one part might wreak subtly pervasive alterations in the rest.[8]

According to this view, there is no purely "sane mind" since the so-called "sane mind" may suffer from temporary emotional disturbances which could cause momentary insanity. This fresh perception of the "sane mind" paradoxically blurred the line that had been supposed to distinguish the sane from the insane, and it demanded a new judicial understanding and legal reform regarding an increasingly pervasive phenomenon in court trials: insanity defense against criminal charges. It provoked an inflamed dispute over legal liability in court between medical men and the defenders of the "unbending dictum of law" in the middle of the century, especially after the publication of Dr. Isaac Ray's *Medical Jurisprudence of Insanity* in 1838 and the formation of the M'Naghten rules in 1843. The M'Naghten rules of England, adopted in the United States in *Commonwealth v. Rogers* (1844), required that, to establish a defense of insanity, "it must be clearly proved that, at the time of the committing of the act, the party accused was labouring under such a defect of reason, from disease of the mind, as not to know the nature and quality of the act he was doing, or, if he did know it, that he did not know he was doing what was wrong."[9]

Dr. Isaac Ray, an outstanding psychiatrist, voiced his strong disagreement with the M'Naghten rules.[10] Ray believed that about ninety percent of asylum patients could distinguish right from wrong "with all their original acuteness." And these criminals, diagnosed as insane by physicians, would be guilty of their criminal acts under the right and wrong test. Ray also criticized the M'Naghten delusion rule, which, he bitterly commented, "revealed a most deplorable ignorance of the mental operations of the insane."[11] Ray advocated that "abstract rules" should be eschewed and that a jury should determine a person's responsibility "by the circumstances of the act in question."[12] The judge should instruct the jury that the question before it was "whether he was insane when he committed the act."[13] Ray felt that it was both socially and legally right to acquit not only those criminals who did not know that their act was wrong but also those who were unable to prevent themselves from committing the act despite the knowledge of its wrongfulness. Ray displayed a wide range of cases where "people of acute reasoning and quick wit were nonetheless demonstrably insane and prone to irresponsible actions."[14] And he categorized insanity as some type of "controlling disease," and the insane people were simply victims of this "controlling disease" and should not be responsible for their behavior or disease.[15] Many other psychiatrists shared similar opinions, addressing this "morbid" but "irresistible impulse" which took "despotic possession" of the patient and drove him to desperate acts in spite of himself.[16]

The opposition from people in legal and other areas to Ray and his supporters, however, was equally strong. At the time, a considerable number of people did not show much trust in psychiatry. Unlike other branches of science which could provide irrefutable concrete proofs and evidence, psychiatry was abstract and abstruse, and it was therefore often mistrusted. Besides, many of these opponents did not agree that insanity should be defined as "a disease," a "controlling disease," or an "irresistible innocent impulse."[17] John P. Gray, the superintendent of the New York Lunatic Asylum at Utica, for example, acknowledged in the late 1850s countless temptations all around a person, but he held the view that man had "an innate ability to choose good over evil" unless that ability was unquestionably disturbed. He believed that those who committed an illegal act were "not sick, but simply immoral."[18] The criminal, according to this judicial opinion, was simply one who succumbed to "perverse inclinations," and he should be assisted but not acquitted by the court. "If you cannot resist an impulse in any other way, we will hang a rope in front of your eyes, and perhaps that will help."[19]

While raising this question "how to determine insanity," *The Gilded Age* also exposes the incompetence and corruption of the court officials and the jury that are authorized to exercise judicial rights. O'Shaunnessy, the judge presiding over the trial, has worked his way from "street Arab" to magistrate via the route of police court politics (487). It is said that he has never had "a lucrative practice nor a large salary," but he has managed to possess lands and houses to "the value of three or four hundred thousand dollars" (487). The corruption of the court has certainly interfered with the whole process of trial, and it is virtually impossible to make an impartial and rational judgment. This can be seen in the empaneling process. The jury, as Braham respectfully addresses them, is composed of "twelve men of rare intelligence, whose acute minds would unravel all the sophistries of the prosecution" (498). In reality, however, most of them are ignorant, illiterate, and incompetent, and only two of them are able to read. Arey Hicks, a peanut peddler, is to be excluded since the prosecuting officer has found out that he is deaf. Nevertheless, Hicks is the very type of person that Braham attempts to empanel because he has seen Hicks looking at Laura "sympathizingly" (492). All of the twelve jurors on the panel have "[l]ow foreheads and heavy faces . . . ; some had a look of animal cunning, while the most were only stupid" (493). Besides, the foreman of the jury is unexpectedly Mr. Braham's friend.

The incompetence and corruption of the court officials and the jury direct our attention to the irrationality in the trial itself. The chief medical expert who testifies that Laura's momentary insanity could be genuine is said to have received "a thousand dollars for looking into the case" (510). When delivering his opening statement, Braham seems highly emotional, and he even pauses as if "overcome by his emotions," even though he is supposed to remain rational and composed (500). His speech, loaded with hyperbole and exaggeration, is designed to appeal to the audience and the jury for their emotional rather than rational response. The novel thus raises this question subtly: Can Braham be sane if he, bribed or simply ignorant, labels a sane Laura as momentarily insane? All of a sudden, the question raised at the very beginning whether or not Laura is insane changes to be whether or not these people at the court are insane. Or how to label these people who are not capable of giving a rational trial of Laura? In either case, money has definitely played a decisive role in the form of bribery in this trial. The irrationality of both the trial and that of the verdict of insanity is directly related to or caused by money.

The epistemological and moral issues that the phenomenon of insanity has raised are pertinent most of all to the novel's dominant aspect—speculation. Twain and Warner have presented to the reader a world of speculation. Nearly all the characters in the novel, including Laura, are involved in speculation. When explaining the social cause of Philip Sterling's mistake, the authors write that Philip "was born into a time when all young men of his age caught the fever of speculation, and expected to get on in the world by the omission of some of the regular processes which have been appointed from of old" (456). It is surely an age of speculation. The widespread "speculative spirit" or "gambling spirit," as William Archibald Dunning commented in 1907, originated from the "hazards and vicissitudes" of the Civil War. After the war, the phenomenon of speculation rapidly and extensively developed because of the unstable general condition of the national finances and the exciting discoveries of some natural resources, such as petroleum in Pennsylvania, the precious metals in the Rocky Mountains, and gold in Montana and Idaho.[20] The "fever of speculation" became a widespread epidemic throughout the country, and nearly everybody became engaged in speculation. It was surely an interestingly distinct period when "presidents were businessmen and generals were businessmen and preachers were businessmen, when the whole psychic energy of the American people was absorbed in the exploitation and organization of the material resources of the continent. . . ."[21]

The word "speculation," first defined by Samuel Johnson in the eighteenth century,[22] attained its new meaning nearly a century later. In the late 1830s, Samuel Maunder, an exceedingly popular English writer, who had witnessed a railway share panic, provided the following definition of the nature of speculation: "The practice of buying articles of merchandise, or any purchasable commodity whatever, in expectation of a rise of price and of selling the same at a considerable advance."[23] Having pointed out the difference between "speculation" and "regular trade," Maunder wrote:

> Speculation on a large scale, upon the principle of monopolising, or that kind of speculation which consists in the purchase and sale of shares in public companies, as well as "dabbling" in the stocks, and a variety of other hazardous transactions which might be named, are different species of gambling and are often no less ruinous.[24]

By naming "speculation" as a "different species of gambling" and "no less ruinous," Maunder both rejected and admitted the notion that speculation is "gambling." As he specified later, unlike gambling, speculation involves "dealing" and requires "artifice" as well as "chance." It is essentially an engagement in risky business transactions for quick or considerable profit.

It is this slippery nature of speculation that somewhat identifies the speculator with the criminal in an insanity defense. Since the speculator often takes the prospective success as a nearby reality, and the promising profit is both imaginary and real, far-away and close-by, the confusion of imagination and reality in the case of speculation is to some degree similar to insanity.

The economic world that *The Gilded Age* has presented is just such a world in which reason and absurdity, or sanity and insanity are intertwined and often indistinguishable. As Van Wyck Brooks stresses, *The Gilded Age* presents a "true folk-Odyssey of our modern civilization," and in this period all its idealism runs into "the channel of money-making."[25] In this pattern of life, all feelings, passions, and emotions are assimilated into "absolute homogeneity of feeling": success.[26] There is only one faith: not in God, but in money. It is true that railway and highway seemed to have shortened the road to success; they made the glorious success more shining and tempting. Silver and gold in California proved that wealth was tangible; they illumined the path with golden prosperity and optimism. Never before had the myth of "manifest destiny" and success been so popular in the country. People like Mark Twain took the "granite rubbish" and "glittering mica" on the ground as pure silver and pure gold, and they forgot that "all that glitters is not gold."[27] The illusion of overnight success through material opportunities shed a light of hope in people's hearts, and motivated John Clemens, Mark Twain's father, to experiment on a perpetual motion machine or Mark Twain to invest feverishly in the Paige automatic typesetting machine. Illusions played the role of stimulant by enhancing a high spirit in people, though many of them failed and were constantly disillusioned.

The Gilded Age continuously exposes and explores this type of confusion and indicates the lack of common logic in the world. A buyer, for example, may offer a price with an intention to be rejected and not to make a business transaction. The stranger from an iron manufacturing company comes to visit Hawkins and offers him ten thousand dollars for his land. When rejected, he says to Hawkins that he has been very straightforward in offering the price "without throwing out any feelers." He tells him, "I did it in the hope that you would refuse" (66-67). His candid refusal to accomplish a transaction appears to Hawkins nothing but a confirmation that he is a shrewd buyer. His candor only evokes Hawkins's suspicion: "This is a deep man; this is a very deep man," and this is "a deep fox . . ." (67). The term "buyer" in this world registers meanings that simultaneously agree with and refuse the conventional logic.

Words and sight are two key elements in speculative activities, and both of them are emphatically highlighted in the novel. Words function as part of the economics, and the wide circulation of words is strikingly salient in the world of speculation in *The Gilded Age*. In their definition of the period, the authors remark:

> Who shall say that this is not the golden age of mutual trust, of unlimited reliance upon human promises? That is a peculiar condition of society which enables a whole nation to instantly recognize point and meaning in the familiar newspaper anecdote, which puts into the mouth of a distinguished speculator in lands and mines this remark:—"I wasn't worth a cent two years ago, and now I owe two millions of dollars." (243)

It is a world of confidence and prosperity, constructed on the base of "mutual trust" and "unlimited reliance upon human promises." Yet the "trust" and "promises" are merely a web of words which often signify a mere delusion for the characters in the novel: Colonel Selby's promise of love and marriage is but a scheme to deflower innocent Laura; Mr. Sellers's rhetoric at the dinner table transforms his humble hut into an illusory magnificent palace; Bigler and Small's projects, which successively fail as there is always "a mistake in figures," always appear well-designed and accomplishable.

In his study of Mark Twain's languages, David Sewell cites Richard Grand White's book *Words and Their Uses* (1870) as an influence on Mark Twain.[28] White, as Sewell points out, noticed the perversion of language in America and believed that it was caused by "the wide diffusion of very superficial instruction among a restless, money-getting, and self-confident people."[29] The brilliance of *The Gilded Age* lies in the fact that the novel has caught the salient feature of that particular historical period by presenting people's unusually faithful reliance upon language. Even though an offer of a price or a name is at its best a verbal promise or a form of recognition, it is often conceived of as an equivalent to a substantial amount of money. A well-known name or an abstract title becomes a sign of high market value. Sellers's title changes from Mr., Major, Captain, to Colonel at various stages of his speculative career, and it is expected to reach up to "General" if he succeeds in the scheme (515). Dilworthy, who is pleased with Laura, addresses her as "my daughter," which instantly transforms Laura's identity and brings her closer to this powerful politician (294). The novel also shows that words are not merely abstract signs, functioning as barometers; they can *be* concrete, and they circulate as money. The distance between appearance and reality or that between the signifier and the signified is apparently eliminated. Words are transformed into the signified. The "high-sounding millionaire names" can be "stuck" in the advertisements as "stockholders." These inanimate names with voices bring money by attracting hundreds and thousands of investors; and in return the service of these "names" costs money since they are "an expensive lot" (257).

But Twain shows again that this frenzied trust in words is not completely devoid of reason. Sellers is surprised when he reads what is said to be his own narration in the newspaper because it has been embellished with the inflated newspaper language. Yet it is in this very inflation and circulation that words have attained their value like money. Even though newspaper English as verbal currency, as White believed, does "not possess the worth its circulators mistakenly ascribe to it,"[30] it may magically generate enormous value if one has a speculative talent and luck. As in Hawkins's case, the weekly Philadelphia newspaper and the semi-weekly St. Louis journal, which provide him with information regarding the "condition of the crops south and east" and the market demand and price, bring him enviable luck and fortune. The clue to this luck is his "brains" that know how to make use of the words.

The bottom line of sanity or insanity lies in the question of perception. A lunatic is blind, unable to distinguish illusion from reality. In his discussion with Washington concerning the potentiality of producing the Infallible Imperial Oriental Optic Liniment and Salvation for Sore Eyes, Sellers makes meticulous calculations to illustrate the rewarding prosperous future when Washington's capital should be accumulated from the present total of eighteen dollars to an annual profit of $350,000. The product of eye water is "the Medical Wonder of the Age," and Sellers will make Washington's money "breed" (87). This project seems so fascinating and promising to Washington that he exclaims with his eyes blazing, "I wish I wasn't cramped and kept down and fettered with poverty, and such prodigious chances lying right here in sight!" (85). He even wishes that the world would "open its eyes" to perceive Sellers's ingenuity.

The world is blind with "sore eyes" both literally and metaphorically, and it does need some magic eye water for treatment, as Harry's case unmistakably confirms. Innocent Harry is rapturous when he reports to Sellers that they have "raked in $200,000 of Uncle Sam's money" without "buying a vote or making a promise." Harry sincerely believes that "if a man knows how to talk to women, and has a little gift in the way of argument with men, he can afford to play for an appropriation against a money bag and give the money bag odds in the game" (228, 229). He feels confident that other people's comments that he is "pretty innocent" or "pretty blind" are unfounded. The truth is unfolded later when he stands in the "Columbus River Slack-Water Navigation Company," confronting a pile of letters and documents:

> "Now here, for instance; do you believe that that is a genuine letter? Do you know this signature here?—and this one? Do you know who those initials represent—and are they forgeries?"
>
> Harry was stupefied. (258)

Harry possesses an extraordinary capacity to identify forgery. Nevertheless, with his confirmation of the genuineness of these signatures, Harry comes to realize his own blindness. "What a stone-blind idiot I have been!" he admits with pain, as he now comprehends the corruption and greed in Congress. This gaining of sight is costly because, rather than acquiring the appropriation of $200,000, Harry and Sellers become debtors, owing $25,000.

The disease of "sore eyes," or blindness, is associated with or largely originates from greed and selfishness. Twain is pessimistic as he believes that, being surrounded and controlled by the motivation of greed, men can never become sharp eyed.[31] The world could only be exploited by such quack doctors as Sellers but never be cured with his eye water. Washington's "recognition" of Sellers's ingenuity is in reality a form of blindness caused by the illusion of enormous profit that Sellers's words have woven. Occasionally, even when someone is fortunate enough to possess a sharp perception, selfishness and egotism make him unwilling to enlighten the world. On his way to Ilium, Philip witnesses the conductor of the train brutally treating a woman passenger. Philip stands up to assist the latter, but he is thrust off the train by the conductor. The following day, the local newspaper publishes the news of this incident in which the conductor's brutal and violent behavior is covered by such euphemistic terms as "courteously," "gently" and "gentlemanly" (265-67). Philip, who has both witnessed the violation of the code on the train and has read the distorting news report in the paper, is aware that it is his "first duty" to "put aside his own business and devote his time and his best efforts to seeing that the infraction is promptly punished." He has also learned from a justice of the peace that the chance for him to win the suit against the railroad company is nearly nonexistent. He is told that "The railroad company owns all these people along here, and the judges on the bench too." He is advised that "least said's soonest mended" (268). An account in another newspaper enables him to see "still more clearly what chance he would have had before the public in a fight with the railroad company" (268). Despite the fact that his conscience urges him to "carry the matter into the courts," he decides to give up the fight. With such a decision, Philip appears to be rational and sharp-eyed; but he is simultaneously and voluntarily blind in the sense that he selfishly relinquishes the conventionally rational sense of "duty" and overlooks the violation of the law "before his own eyes" (268, 269).

Among the major characters in the novel, Sellers is indisputably the most frantic speculator. His language, which often expresses his confidence in success and stimulates other people's desire for upward mobility, is in many cases both sane and insane. His tongue, as Twain writes, was "a magician's wand that turned dried apples into figs and water into wine as easily as it could change a hovel into a palace and present poverty into imminent future riches" (83). With his tongue, the poverty-stricken life can be transformed into an enjoyment or something desirable. At the dinner table, with his explanation to Washington, "lowly potatoes" become products of "some ducal garden" supervised by the duke himself, and the seemingly "execrable" coffee, said to be brought from the "private stores of a Brazilian nobleman," becomes a "lingering luxury" (83). Like the supper, the breakfast is "transformed into an oriental feast" (84). Sellers gives a rationale for any illusion his tongue has weaved. The fact that he cannot afford to purchase mustard becomes in his explanation to Washington an intentional refusal to have mustard: "I'm a plain man, and I want my food plain. . . . [H]igh living kills more than it cures in this world" (110-11). And he convinces Washington that water and turnips are "full of nutriment," and they guarantee the resistance of the plague in the future (111).

Sellers is "the visionary,"[32] and he constantly maps the future prosperity. However, his designs, always coated with reason and logic, can never be carried out in reality. His plan for constructing the town of Napoleon, for example, attempts to straighten, deepen, and widen the Columbus River near Stone's Landing. His optimism is high as usual, and his method of development is logical and feasible. Sellers and Harry move along with "the air of men who had been charged with the work of altering the foundation of the globe" (230). Unfortunately, his scheme to acquire an appropriation from Congress fails, and his grand project is thus aborted, this time because of the shortage of funds. The project could be completed and the map become true if the Congress were not corrupt and the appropriation was granted. Sellers is the man who lives in the "realm of possibility," and he demonstrates some Quixotic courage to attempt successive experiments for money making.[33] In other words, Sellers's optimism and sanity may be regarded as a special form of insanity because he takes as virtually real the "realm of possibility," which is not always identical with reality.

The character of Sellers raises a complicated moral issue regarding the nature of his deeds. The novel shows that Sellers's insanity, coated with rationality and reason, can be dangerous to individuals and society. With an air of generosity and affection, Sellers peddles his ideas and repeatedly causes other people's misfortunes. He "nearly ruined" the Hawkinses at first by endeavoring to help them make their fortune, and he then "crippled" them in Kentucky. At the beginning of the novel, he is again trying to persuade the Hawkinses to move further west to Missouri for participation in his "biggest scheme on earth" (29). Money is his only concern. For the sake of money, he can despise or manipulate the law. Before the Civil War, he devised a scheme to buy the black people and send them down to the South while he tried to "get a law made stopping everybody from selling negroes to the south after a certain day." By this, he planned to raise the price of the black slave up to four times. His scheme tumbled as the law did not pass. After the War, he holds on to his prejudice against this "emancipated race" and tries to make profit out of the black people. By claiming that the black people are "a speculating race . . . disinclined to work for white folks without security," he denies them the legitimate opportunity to receive an education and makes them an object of his speculation (187). In the meantime, Sellers manipulates the black people by having them sign the petition for improving the navigation of the Columbus River, a petition which would bring economic advantage to the Hawkinses and himself. Sellers's expertise in rhetoric helps him enhance his attractiveness and credibility when he actually deserves condemnation for his irrational and immoral decisions and acts. Sellers, or his insanity, is a representative part of the disturbing forces in this social and economic world.

Yet there is another side of Sellers which may qualify him as innocent, generous, and morally sound. Sellers has "splendid ideas" and is always willing to "divide his chances with his friends with a free hand, the good generous soul" (27). He helps the Hawkinses, and extends a warm welcome to Philip Sterling and Henry Brierly when they get to his town. "Nobody can help liking the creature, he means so well," as Mrs. Hawkins frankly admits. With his many seemingly rational but actually insane explanations, Sellers does not mean to anesthetize his audience. As a matter of fact, his words often function as a stimulant of encouragement. Built upon the base of irrationality and illogicality, these romantic illusions, woven with his words, are vital in sustaining and enhancing the morale of the explorers such as Washington, Harry, or Philip in their search for wealth, and supporting them to "overcome hostile influences."[34]

While Sellers is the most frantic speculator in the novel, Laura Hawkins may be considered as the most intricate among all the characters. Though the court holds a debate on whether or not she was insane momentarily at the murder scene, the novel suggests that the rationality of her actions prior to that was no less questionable. Unlike those women who remain stable in their social positions, Laura is endowed with "the fatal gift of beauty" (169), which adds up to her "power of fascination" and assists her later in her lobbying at the Congress. At home, she indulges herself in reading romances and other books by Byron, Scott, and Shelley, which feed her imagination with "the most exaggerated notions of life." Like other speculators, she likes to contemplate a possible ideal outcome (e.g., what should a woman with beauty and fascination expect to obtain from society) and she has formulated "a very false sort of heroism" in the cause of women's liberation (172). She is blind in reality since she cannot see through Selby, a married Confederate officer who seduces her and then tramples her. She "did not or would not see" any faults and selfishness in Selby, and she marries and gives herself "utterly to her husband" until she is abandoned by him[35] (174-75).

Laura's experience with Selby brings her a painful realization of her poverty, a keen apprehension of her rich possession of the "gifts" for potential success, and an unquenchable desire for power and revenge. The same factors transform Laura into a dreamer.

> Laura had her dreams. She detested the narrow limits in which her lot was cast, she hated poverty. Much of her reading had been of modern works of fiction, written by her own sex, which had revealed to her something of her own powers and given her indeed, an exaggerated notion of the influence, the wealth, the position a woman may attain who has beauty and talent and ambition and a little culture, and is not too scrupulous in the use of them. She wanted to be rich, she wanted luxury. (181-82)

Laura comes to perceive that she may use her "beauty and talent and ambition and a little culture" to obtain "wealth" and "luxury." She yearns to gain wealth and power regardless of the means, and she desires to exercise her power over men. Though being more perceptive and apprehensive now, Laura, similar to Sellers, has failed to ponder over a fine but crucial part in her project. In her case, she has failed to distinguish "the nicest discrimination between notoriety and reputation" (182). Laura is never aware that notoriety can be fatal to a woman who attempts to conquer and occupy a stronghold in this world of speculation. There is a stream of speculators flowing into the capital: Washington comes to the capital for the Tennessee Land; Sellers and Harry for the Stone Landing; and Selby, as the victim of the war, for the cotton claim (352). Along with the stream rushes Laura, motivated with a similar economic desire.

Laura is shown to be extraordinarily clear-minded and shrewd in her battle in Washington. As an influential and sophisticated lobbyist, she is keen-sighted, able to perceive bribery and see through illusion. She knows the most important characters in the capital. She visits "the Aristocracy of the Parvenus" and receives calls from important officials. She quickly familiarizes herself with "'society' customs" (296) and observes the language and rules. Soon after she has arrived in Washington, Laura becomes widely admired. "Ministers, Generals, Congressman, and all manner of aristocratic people" surround her wherever she goes. She can tell the discrepancy between the printed words on Balloon's boxes and their contents (331-34). She sees clearly the bribery and knavery of the Congressmen and shows her expertise in using these facts as a means to blackmail them (378-79). And her extraordinary sight is rarely blotted by temporary success. When Washington is intoxicated in dreaming the potential gain of the "millions," she derides him and awakens him to reality: "You never wait till the foremost dollar of it arrives within a hundred miles of you" (319).

With her clear sight and a good mastery of language, Laura's voice is quickly heard in Congress. As she herself has predicted, ". . . if one may judge by what she hears, there are chances" for "a fascinating woman" (275). She becomes a lobbyist and a speaker. She is the ghost writer of the eloquent speech that Trollop delivers at the Congress supporting the Indigent Congressmen's Retroactive Appropriation. She proudly reveals to Trollop, "*I* wrote your speech myself, and you read it from my manuscript" (382). The success of Trollop's speech stands as a proof that Laura's voice has been subtly and smoothly transfused into the Congress. She has mastered the rules and strategy of its political game. She schemes to manipulate Trollop and have him do her "a good turn" by influencing the vote of the bill for the Tennessee Land in Congress.

Nevertheless, her clear-mindedness or sanity is undermined by the fact that she often fails to apprehend the massive opposition of her opponents. After her bargain with Trollop, Laura, though nervous about the pending vote, complacently regards Trollop as "a coward" and believes that she has managed to put Trollop under her control. She fails to see that Trollop, a crafty politician, is not so easy to be subjugated. He is, in fact, to "contrive something fresh to get back to Congress" (388). Besides, Laura places her hope on Selby, who she mistakenly believes would elope with her to Europe if her bribery were exposed and her reputation ruined (389).

Laura comes to Washington as a victim of the Civil War. She is "ruined" and has become "a soiled cast-off" (351). She looks for "love."

But it is precisely this obstinate desire for "love" that puts Laura's mental and moral states into question. Years earlier when she was abandoned by Selby, Laura "wanted to be rich, she wanted luxury, she wanted men at her feet, her slaves" (181-82). This very notion of becoming a slave-master of "men" accompanies her into the capital, and it is there even in these questions about her love relationship with Selby: "Had she not a right to him? Did he not belong to her by virtue of her overmastering passion?" (353).

The novel suggests that the Civil War, which was over in 1865, has been transformed into a new form of battle in the capital of the country. The former enmity between the North and the South has melted, and the former conflicts in economic interests and all forces have been consolidated under the banner of "For success." As Mrs. Schoonmaker complacently explains to Laura about the ameliorated present situation:

> "You know we don't say 'rebel' anymore. Before we came to Washington I thought rebels would look unlike other people. I find we are very much alike, and that kindness and good nature wear away prejudice. And then you know there are all sorts of common interests. My husband sometimes says that he doesn't see but confederates are just as eager to get at the treasury as Unionists." (347)

Despite Schoonmaker's claim of a peaceful and harmonious sphere, war terminology, reminiscent of the Civil War, occurs incessantly. It is not incidental for Laura to raise the question of the "rebel element" in her conversation with Mrs. Schoonmaker since Laura has been engaged in the economic battle of speculation ever since her arrival in Washington. While on one side of the battle is the single-handed Laura representing the anger of the females, on the other are Selby, Buckstone, Trollop, and other congressmen representing the males.[36]

To some extent, Laura stands for the cause of justice. She is a fighter for the rights of women, including Ruth, Alice, and herself. She is also an avenger. Every victory instantly brings back to her "the bitter day that Col. Selby trampled her love and her pride in the dust" (316). And she links her battle there with the cause of the whole female gender as she says to Harry: "I'm angry with the cruel world, which pursues an independent woman as it never does a man" (365). Laura dallies with the admirers of her wealth and her beauty. When some of "the noblest men of the time succumbed to worship her," Laura simply "enthralled" them by first not frowning upon them and then flatly turning them down. Each of those frustrated lovers would "go away hating and cursing the whole sex, and she would calmly add his scalp to her string" (316). By exciting men's hopes and then denying them, inflating their passion and then restraining it, Laura enjoys "keen delight" since it proves that "she had power over men" (183).

However, Laura's excessive and nearly uncontrollable desire for revenge and domination has transformed her formerly innocent self into a potentially destructive element in the socioeconomic system. With her extraordinary "power of fascination," Laura arouses the fever of speculation among all her suitors.[37] With her popularity increasing daily, Laura will soon have her own pockets filled with "millions of money." She is thus considered wealthy and expected to be "vastly more so in a little while" by selling the Tennessee Lands (316). With her possessions ever increasing, Laura becomes an even more desirable object of speculation. But Laura, with her beauty and wealth, traps her admirers. One man after another falls victim to her. Buckstone, a Congressman, "diligently continued his effort to win her," but before long he finds himself held in leash with a line of "conspicuous captives."

> These unfortunates followed Laura helplessly, for whenever she took a prisoner he remained her slave henceforth. Sometimes they chafed in their bondage; sometimes they tore themselves free and said their serfdom was ended; but sooner or later they always came back penitent and worshipping. (372)

The familiar terminology, such as "slave," "bondage," and "serfdom," suggests a revival of the recently abolished slavery system. Laura's justified cause to fight for the rights of women is repeatedly undermined by the threatening potentiality that her "power of fascination" may convert the whole male sex into self-enslaved slaves.

Laura, by lobbying, bargaining, and menacing, also constitutes a notorious threat to the normal function of Congress. In order to pass the Knobs University Bill, which can lead to the sale of the Tennessee lands, she lobbies Buckstone and many other Congressmen. To secure the necessary votes, she contrives a scheme to subjugate Trollop, a bitter enemy of the Bill, into agreeing to vote for the Bill. Laura secretly prepares for Trollop a speech, which gives the latter his "eloquence" and helps to pass his favored Soldiers' Pension Bill. In return, Laura, with blackmail, threatening, and bribery, cunningly bargains with Trollop to win his support of the Knobs University Bill (379-85).

> "I would much rather talk about my bill."
> "So would I, now, my clandestine amanuensis. Compared with some other subjects, even your bill is a pleasant topic to discuss."
> "Very good indeed! I thought I could persuade you. Now I am sure you will be generous to the poor negro and vote for that bill."
> "Yes, I feel more tenderly toward the oppressed colored man than I did. Shall we bury the hatchet and be good friends and respect each other's little secrets, on condition that I vote Aye on the measure?"
> "With all my heart, Mr. Trollop. I give you my word of that."
> "It is a bargain. But isn't there something else you could give me, too?" (385).

The Bill, in Trollop's term, is a fraud upon the government" (377). As Trollop agrees to reconcile and be Laura's ally, the Bill will be passed to serve Laura's and Congressmen's interests. The proposed University, designed to provide educational opportunities to the colored people, has been so arranged in secrecy that it will be a channel for the Congressmen to line their relatives' pockets so-called "benefit." The loudly manifested interests in the blacks are nothing but a mask to cover the deal that benefits these speculators.

The novel, with Laura's insanity appeal at the pivot, thus presents a picture of social insanity, yet it also raises a difficult moral issue, that is, how to dispose Laura and how to eliminate this social phenomenon of insanity. Paradoxically, moral concern and realism are integrally connected with this issue. A realistic presentation is inevitably colored by the authors' subjective inclination and moral concern with the socioeconomic order.

Twain and Warner emphasize repeatedly that this novel is not a fiction but a text of history. It is a mimetic presentation of reality (5, 524, 525, 576). Or as the subtitle indicates, "A Tale of Today."[38] In claiming their realistic and true-to-fact stance and their accurate transcription of reality, the authors try to set up a standard to differentiate fiction from history: history stands for an accurate, impartial presentation of reality as it actually is; fiction, often sentimental, subjective and fabricated, is colored with moral admonishing. Traditional sentiment, fabricated dramatic plots, conventional expectations—all these fictitious fabrications should be selectively reduced or entirely excised since they are rarely encountered in life. And the novel, as literary historian Everett Carter comments, launches an "attack in fiction upon sentimentalism in literature. . . ."[39] As if the reader needs to be constantly reminded, the authors interpolate their advice repeatedly to demarcate reality from fiction and to prepare the reader for "disappointments" at such moments when the chairman of the House Committee fails to appear or when Laura's father is nowhere to be seen. Such "disappointments," though they "seldom occur in novels," are always happening in real life" and are signs of realistic presentation (335).

Yet the authors' claim of a realistic stance is being challenged, particularly by their very apology or explication in Chapter 58 where the verdict is delivered. Soon after the Jury has announced the verdict "NOT GUILTY" and the "kissing of Braham" scene has taken place, the judge delivers his sentence.

> "In accordance with the directions of the law in such cases," said the Judge, "and in obedience to the dictates of a wise humanity, I hereby commit Laura Hawkins to the care of the Superintendent of the State Hospital for Insane Criminals, to be held in confinement until the State Commissioners on Insanity shall order her discharge. Mr. Sheriff, you will attend at once to the execution of this decree." (523)

The Judge's decision, based on the fact that Laura, with an unsound mind, would be "dangerous to the safety of the community," may eliminate one element of violence and disturbance, but it arouses panic in Laura's otherwise released soul. "Laura insane! And about to be locked up with madmen!" Laura is quickly transported to the hospital for lunatic criminals, and she is shocked by the imminent scenario of being locked in a "small, bare room" and confronting all "the horrible creatures" with their "dreadful faces." She attempts to convince the physician at the hospital that she is "not insane;" yet her belief is soon replaced by the doubt "if she *were* not mad." Confronted with such a gruesome reality of prison life, Laura feels that it is better "to have died, than to slowly go mad in this confinement" (524). At this very critical juncture appears the authorial apology:

> —We beg the reader's pardon. This is not history, which has just been written. It is really what would have occurred if this were a novel. If this were a work of fiction, we should not dare to dispose of Laura otherwise. True art and any attention to dramatic proprieties required it.

> The novelist who would turn loose upon society an insane murderess could not escape condemnation. Besides, the safety of society, the decencies of criminal procedure, what we call our modern civilization, all would demand that Laura should be disposed of in the manner we have described. (524-25)

Hence, the Judge's verdict, Laura's panic, and her pending confinement mentioned above are merely scenes for a fiction or simply an illusion. What the authors intend to present here is "history," a satirical but accurate picture of reality where there is no such law to detain Laura, no such hospital for insane criminals, and no such "State Commission of Lunacy" (525).

This apology, though designed to set a clear distinction between history and fiction and to serve as a reminder of the authors' realistic stance, becomes a challenge as it reveals the authors' moral concern and indicates a suppressed wish or even the possible confusion of the authors. The scenario mentioned above underlines that confining Laura to a mental hospital is a moral execution, which could secure the safety of the community and benefit "our modern civilization." However, as the authors unwillingly acknowledge, this moral execution, which only "a work of fiction" would understandably carry out, has to be sacrificed to favor the interest of realism. But the scenario is presented in such a manner—with its fast pace, a joyful tone, and a sarcastic revelation of a guilty but sane Laura—that it seems almost as if the authors indulged their emotions and were carried away by their moral concerns. While Mrs. Hawkins falls in a "stupor" as she is struck with the unexpected familial calamity, the authors seem to have also fallen in a "stupor," outlining a fictitious but moral execution of Laura. Hence, the authorial apology following this scenario is simultaneously an apology for their mishap in reverie and a moral condemnation of the acquitted criminal as well. Yet with all these considered, the apology makes the claim of a realistic stance suspected.

Twain was furious against the insanity defense, and voiced his rage at the acquittal of the criminals in some insanity defense cases in "A New Crime," a short story written around 1870. The story presents and comments on a couple of "the most remarkable" cases of insanity, in which the accused murderers successfully escape from the punishment with exculpatory insanity. In one case, Baldwin, the accused, is said to have insulted a "helpless cripple," who in turn knocked him down. Two days later, Baldwin goes and shoots him dead. The defense attorney argues that Baldwin was insane "at half-past ten in the morning on the day of the murder, and remained so for eleven hours and a half exactly." Since the time period of insanity covered the case, the accused is acquitted. Twain writes, "The Baldwins were very wealthy." The same Baldwin commits murder twice afterwards, but with his family's political influence and money he is twice acquitted. Twain exclaims that insanity is "on the increase" while crime is "dying out" in the world. The punishment of the law can no longer reach criminals who have money and power. Near the end of the story, Twain appeals to the public for "a law against *insanity*." He stresses that it is in insanity "where the true evil lies,"[40] and urges that the criminals should be accordingly punished.

Nevertheless, Twain is aware that in a realistic novel or play, a moral and ideal execution has to be sacrificed in order to give a realistic treatment of the subject. On September 16, 1874, the opening night of the play *The Gilded Age*, adapted by Twain, he delivered a speech with a discussion of this particular issue.

> If a play carries its best lesson by teaching what ought to be done in such a case, but is *not* done in real life, then the righteous verdict of guilty should appear; but if the best lesson may be conveyed by holding up the mirror and showing what *is* done every day in such a case but ought *not* to be done, then the satirical verdict of not guilty should appear.[41]

In the play, the Jury's verdict of "not guilty" is retained. With this change, Twain is carrying out the realistic principle while he is conscious of "what ought to be done" but is "*not* done" in real life.

It is through their very conscious effort to maintain a realistic stance that the authors' unquenchable desire to realign the social order by correcting the phenomenon of insanity in both the economic system and the insanity defense becomes perceivable. Yet this manifest desire often interferes and tempts them to perform a moral correction, and the novel thus occasionally deviates from its "realistic" stance. The sharp distinction between what "ought to be done" and what "ought *not* to be done" in real life appears blurred in the mirror because the novel implicitly suggests what "ought to be done" in order to correct the phenomenon of insanity. In other words, in their presenting an objective history of the time, Twain and Warner perform as economists,[42] arranging and distributing economic rewards and punishments. And by thus doing, they become unconsciously involved. All these can be seen in the authorial arrangement of the characters and the plot development, which are an undeniably subjective management to bring about economic order and stabilization.

The novel introduces the lives of two distinctively different young female characters: Ruth Bolton and Laura Hawkins. The two women share many similarities in regard to their discontent with women's social status. Laura aspires to be a contender in the heroic cause of emancipation of women; Ruth struggles to break "the cage of custom," try the limits of the social order, and "re-arrange the world" (138). She is not content to stay in "the box" that society has set up for her. She wants "to be something" and "to do something" (137). And for this very reason, she is determined to study medical science at Fallkill.

Yet, despite this feature of rebellious discontent they share, there is a fundamental difference between the two in terms of sanity. As Philip quite joyfully detects, Ruth, in spite of her playfulness and seemingly nonchalant attitude, has "the airy grace of sanity" (371). Unlike Laura, Ruth never indulges herself in reading romance, old poetry or the latest novel; she reads "reports of clinics" (241). She studies to be a medical scientist, one who cultivates rationality by curing insanity, while Laura's scheme and sophisticated rhetoric only aggravate insanity in the economic and political spheres. Ruth has a "shield" against any sentiment (371), which keeps her from being aberrant. And this shield also helps her align her views with reason and sobriety. Because of her sanity, Ruth's vision is consistently clear. She observes the restrictions that men have unfairly imposed on educated women, who are thus supposedly just "petted and supported" and unable "to earn an honest living by their own exertions." As she says to Philip, ". . . you would all choose to have me stay idly at home, and give up my profession" (438).

It seems most puzzling that Ruth, at the very moment when "she was never more certain that she was right and she was sufficient unto herself" (462), unexpectedly changes her mind and shows her willingness to compromise by giving up her medical career in order to secure a stable familial relationship. Yet Ruth's compromise with, or rather her surrender to, Philip here renders precisely a proof of her sanity since she comprehends the harsh and insane opposition to a professional woman from all social relationships. She has lost her passion for freedom and a medical career. She is "tired" and willing to meet her father's prediction that "women won't hold out long." And she even questions the validity of her fight for equality of power in the past and recognizes the need of Philip's tender "sympathy" (462-63). In her compromise, however, her past efforts to be self-sufficient qualify her as a better wife. Ruth has now become a woman similar to thousands of others. To be more accurate, Ruth has become another Alice, a conventional submissive woman, willing to give up exploring her own potential and to bear sufferings for the sake of love. But Ruth is more capable than Alice, who simply bears her burden "alone," "with a self-renunciation and heroism of which men, impatient and complaining, had no conception" (457). As "a pretty physician," Ruth is able to serve Philip, make Philip sober, and "coax" him "to live through almost anything" (283).

The authors' misgivings about the new women's unconventional ideas and values are displayed here in Ruth's ultimate surrender and her return to the rank of the conventional women. To Mark Twain, women are supposed to make a home for men. In his letter to Mollie Fairbanks on February 9, 1876, for example, Twain makes it explicit that women's role at the domestic realm is essential and respectable. He first lays out his opinion of an ideal woman, and he then begins to comment on Mollie Fairbanks's house, which is described as a feminine edifice: designed by Mollie's mother and built "out of the solid rock" of Mollie's "nature." The house can be turned into "a gaudy & unrestful Palace of Sham," but when properly managed, Twain remarks, it may be "a Home—a refuge, a place where the eye is satisfied, the intellect stimulated, the spirit broadened, the soul surcharged with peace."[43] It is noticeable that Twain uses the image of house metaphorically to suggest that women should be "accommodating," like a house providing shelter for men who suffer from insecurity, uncertainty, or disappointment in society. They should not be "playful," "with a shield;" still less should they be manipulative. Women ought to provide men with sincerity and tranquility, qualities that Alice and Ruth have shown in their treatment of Philip. And this relationship seems to be naturalized by the satirical comment that Ruth's compromise, or surrender, is "the riddle as old as creation" (463).

Furthermore, women's domestic assistance is shown to be essential in constructing economic order, both domestic and societal. Those women who are untainted by pecuniary desire or speculative passion in the novel possess a sane instinct, which is an antidote to the economic problems and a safety valve in the economic system. At the beginning of the novel, for example, Nancy Hawkins instinctively senses the danger of Sellers's speculative scheme as soon as her husband, excited with the grandiose investment opportunity in Missouri, mentions the name "Sellers." While Sellers's eloquent rhetoric and beautiful imagination have repeatedly attracted and trapped his credulous followers, Mrs. Hawkins never regards Sellers as "right well balanced" (27), and she dreads to "come across him again," even though he is popular and likeable. She warns her husband that Sellers is "bound to set us all crazy" (29), a prediction which proves to be true later. Similarly, Mrs. Bolton shows her sagacity in welcoming the "misfortune" that her family have to "give up" their house and the land. She regards it as "the least of misfortunes": "We were never happier than when we were in a much humbler home," a life away from endless "anxiety" in dealing with the "beautiful demon of Money" (446, 447).

In Ruth's compromise, the contrast between Ruth and Laura becomes even sharper. Laura fights for women's rights. However, in demanding love from Selby, she paradoxically becomes "the champion of the wrongs of her sex" rather than the champion of her sex (430). Her tenacity in rebellion and her mastery of the political rhetoric set her apart from all other women and make her antagonistic to men. She would never agree to play the role of a submissive woman. Even after her release, Laura, whose love is "forfeited," endeavors to maintain her status of being a fascinating woman by lecturing in order to obtain "fame," "admiration," and "the applause of the multitude" (547). She dreams of making lecture tours from city to city "like a queen of romance." While the public is alarmed by this spiteful woman and her "proposed discourse" and the papers are loaded with comments on this "shameless murderer," "brazen lobbyist," and "heartless seducer," Laura feels even more passionate and determined than ever to prove to the world her capability. Decorated with fine attire and jewels, she uses her eloquence to "enchant" the audience and her "unapproachable beauty" to "amaze" the general public. In contrast to Ruth, who is rational and stable, Laura lives an irrational life of "rapturous intoxications" and is haunted with an awareness of homelessness.

Nevertheless, Laura's life is soon afterwards terminated by Twain's "*boss* chapter": she dies from a heart attack after her first unsuccessful lecture attempt.[44] Twain's reference to the dead Laura "as dead as a mackerel" might sound flippant, but it does not amount to "a lack of seriousness" in his execution.[45] Instead, the death of Laura, who has become an agitator and an element of disturbance, reveals Mark Twain's serious concern for social stabilization and economic sanity. By relieving Laura from the criminal charges and then terminating her life with a heart attack, Twain successfully maintains his posture as a realistic writer while having his moral concern satisfied.

A moral execution in the narrative concerning this world of insanity can also be traced in the development and outcome of the plot itself. The story has three plot lines entangling and developing simultaneously: Sellers's project of the Columbus River and Napoleon, the Hawkinses' Tennessee Land, and Philip's and the Boltons' Ilium land. All three projects are aimed at making enormous fortunes, but all the entrepreneurs eventually either have to or choose to give up their ownership after recognizing that the golden prosperity of their speculation is illusory. However, Sellers's and the Hawkinses' projects have some significant differences from Philip's: both Sellers and the Hawkinses get Congress involved and attempt to obtain funds from Congress; both resort to such illegal means as bribery, cheating, or blackmail; they both manipulate the interests of the black people as a political banner in order to gain their own economic "success," though they have no genuine interest in helping the black people. On the other hand, Philip's project, though speculative like the other two, neither covets favor from Congress and the legislature nor resorts to other illegal means. Philip toils with his workmen in the tunnel of the mine, searching for the coal vein. Even after his disappointed employees have all left him, he remains there, drilling and fighting his battle alone.

All these entrepreneurs fail financially near the end of the novel, yet their failure turns out to suggest a gain of true fortune. The concept of richness, in Mark Twain's view, is always relative: a poor man can be rich if he is content and happy with his material inadequacy and financial destitution; a millionaire such as Cornelius Vanderbilt, who owns seventy million, can be hopelessly and miserably suffering from "poverty" since he needs five hundred million to be truly rich. In other words, wealth "consists in being satisfied with what one has, not in having a great deal and always wanting more."[46] Contentedness with a simple life may thus be viewed as some special form of precious possession. The comment on the effect of the boat explosion accident on the Hawkinses near the beginning of the novel is a recapitulation of the same concept: ". . . the Hawkinses were richer by twenty-four hours of experience in the contemplation of human suffering and in learning through honest hard work how to relieve it" (53). In this sense, all the three entrepreneurs end up being rich precisely because of their failures: Sellers finally discovers his "native element" and the path to success (557). Washington recognizes that the land confers no "happiness" but a "curse" to the family, and that they have been foolishly chasing butterflies. After Washington gives up the land, "the life-long curse is ended" (556-59), and the long-lost freedom regained. As for Philip, he discerns "how much poorer he was by possessing it," and he transfers back to the Boltons the ownership of the land in which he finally discovers a coal mine (452). By giving the land away, Philip devotes himself to Ruth and wins Ruth's love, an even richer mine.

In the novelists' attributing different rewards and retribution to the characters with the outcome of the plot, a moral judgment and an economic design are at once accomplished. The novel is concluded with this statement: "The end of a thing is better than the beginning." The statement is really a claim of multiple achievements: an impartial distribution of rewards and retributions, a neat arrangement of the plot, and an accurate presentation of history. Yet, it is in the very ending of this novel that we perceive that the seemingly "impartial" is actually "partial," "neat" is "uneven," and "accurate" is "subjective." All these are particularly perceptible in the Ilium project which has finally succeeded in the end: the coal mine turns out "even better than was at first hoped" and, if judiciously managed, can be a substantial fortune to both Philip, who retains contentedly only a "share" of it, and the Boltons (572).

Conventional morality is being noticeably prescribed as a cure for the "controlling disease." Philip's fever of speculation is cured by the Jeffersonian bucolic life. And he revives Ruth miraculously by allaying her "fever" contracted in the hospital (571). The couple then enjoy "the pure air of the highlands, amid the golden glories of ripening September."

> Mere life is a luxury, and the color of the grass, of the flowers, of the sky, the wind in the trees, the out-lines of the horizon, the forms of clouds, all give a pleasure as exquisite as the sweetest music to the ear famishing for it. The world was all new and fresh to Ruth, as if it had just been created for her, and love filled it, till her heart was overflowing with happiness. (573)

If "sane," as suggested by its Latin origin *sanus*, stands for "healthy," the "new and fresh" world, filled with "love" and idyllic atmosphere, breeds sanity in Ruth and Philip (573-74). Wealth and money have lost their temptation to the couple; or the conventional concepts of "wealth" and "happiness" have been replaced with a fresh meaning. Instead of pursuing material success, the couple enjoy their life in the country, simple yet rich with "a great deal of love" which they can "spare" for their beloved ones (574).

The form of the novel—its arrangement of the characters and the plot development—seems to have solved the social problem by bringing sanity to society in a hopeful and rose-colored ending. But this very solution is purely idealistic as it simply covers up the difficulties in curing and preventing the social phenomenon of insanity. It leaves some serious questions unanswered, such as how to eliminate or prevent the corruption at the legislature and how to prevent the future Dilworthies, Trollops or Buckstones from gaining power. In Sellers's optimistic statements, "I've seen enough to show me where my mistake was," and "I'm going to begin again" (557), it can be sensed that restlessness and insane passion are still active in Sellers. If Sellers becomes a lawyer in the future, he may constitute an even greater threat to society. The germ of insanity is clearly in the vision here. Sellers's hope to rise in the future from a practicing lawyer to "Chief Justice of the Supreme Court of the United States" is, therefore, less an expression of optimism than an indication of the possible repetition of the false hope in the future (558). The disposition of Laura, who is both a sexual and female scapegoat for the insane speculation in society, means no more than an eradication of a disturbing force in the social and economic system and a temporary amelioration of the situation.

The incompleteness of the solution both manifests the novelists' effort in searching for a complete and satisfactory one to the problem and confirms the difficulty they have confronted. In the trial scene, the Judge,

Braham, Mrs. Hawkins, and the jury, who try to search for "the origin of an aberration of mind" in order to diagnose accurately its nature and prescribe a good solution, find their search futile since Laura's real father, possibly a lunatic, is nowhere to be found (501). Similarly, the novel returns to the same subject of Laura's origin in its Appendix at the very end:

> Perhaps some apology to the reader is necessary in view of our failure to find Laura's father. We supposed, from the ease with which lost persons are found in novels, that it would not be difficult. But it was; indeed, it was impossible; and therefore the portions of the narrative containing the record of the search have been stricken out. (576)

Twain and Warner seem to be defending their realistic stance here as they claim that realistic writers should not invent an origin for Laura. However, this statement circumvents the real problem, not one of epistemology, but that of the authorial ambivalence towards the power of money and the fever of speculation.

Twain's ambivalence toward the power of money and the fever of speculation has clearly predestined the futility of his efforts: he condemned money, which had usurped the sacred throne of God, but the despised money was his very dream, a dream that he pursued all his life. He ridiculed the frenzied speculative fever contaminating his contemporaries and refused to exploit the Tennessee Land his father had left for the family to make fortunes, but he was always an inventor, investor, promoter, and publisher, chasing the hallucinatory rainbows' promise of gold and fortunes. He could devote about fifteen years and two hundred thousand dollars to Paige's machine, a long-term, expensive dream that was, in William Dean Howells's words, "practically impracticable."[47] And he would boast, not without regret, in *Life on the Mississippi*, "The first time I ever saw St. Louis I could have bought it for six million dollars and it was the mistake of my life that I did not do it."[48] Twain's inconsistency, ambivalence, and idiosyncratic passion were not sudden impulses; they were life-long traits of this legendary character. These traits should not be categorized as individual attributes; they were really societal, shared by the whole generation in every part of the country. His mistakes and failures in investments did not stem from miscalculations; they came, rather, from a sharp perception of the beckoning of the magic money. Nowhere has Twain's ambivalence toward money and the speculativeness of the Gilded Age revealed itself more clearly than his following statement in the preface to the first London edition of the novel:

> In America nearly every man has his dream, his pet scheme, whereby he is to advance himself socially or pecuniarily. It is this all-pervading speculativeness which we have tried to illustrate in "The Gilded Age." It is a characteristic which is both bad and good, for both the individual and the nation. Good, because it allows neither to stand still, but drives both forever on, toward some point or other which is a-head, not behind nor at one side. Bad, because the chosen point is often badly chosen and then the individual is wrecked; the aggregation of such cases affects the nation, and so is bad for the nation. Still, it is a trait which it is of course better for a people to have and sometimes suffer from than to be without.[49]

Twain suggests explicitly that speculativeness, while being disastrous and perturbing, is not notoriously negative. Instead, it may have constituted a progressive social force, transfusing energy and vitality into the body of the nation.[50] For this reason, to eradicate this predominant trait of insanity, to Twain, could only be a daunting task, no less than crashing the optimistic dreams of the Gilded Age.

Again this echoes the above mentioned epistemological and moral issues raised by the insanity defense. The difficulty that Twain and Warner have confronted in their execution of the plot and characters was undeniably great. Nevertheless, it is because of their ambivalence toward this epidemic "controlling disease" and it is because of the very incompleteness of the solution that the authors have succeeded in presenting to the world an accurate vista of the Gilded Age.

Chapter II

Economy of Sympathy: *A Hazard of New Fortunes*

William Dean Howells's *A Hazard of New Fortunes* begins with the famous house-hunting scene in New York. Basil March and his wife, having visited several apartment houses for a "dwelling of some sort," are disappointed in either the exorbitant rent or the poor condition of the apartment. The house-hunting experience is so confusing and exhausting that the Marches unintentionally visit twice the house owned by a widow who has a daughter to support and wants to take the Marches to board. Later that day Basil suggests to his wife that, if they are truly humane, they should modify their desires to meet the needs of the widow and end this "sickening search."

> "Yes; but we're *not* truly humane," his wife answered, "or at least not in that sense. You know you hate boarding; and if we went there I should have them on my sympathies the whole time."
>
> "I see. And then you would take it out of me."
>
> "Then I should take it out of you. And if you are going to be so weak, Basil, and let every little thing work upon you in that way, you'd better not come to New York. You'll see enough misery here."[1]

Careful preservation and frugal utilization of sympathy seem to be a primary concern on Isabel March's agenda. Even in Boston, before leaving for New York, she expresses the same concern to her husband. "New York terrifies me," she confesses to her husband. The city, with a population of two million, seems intimidating. "I'm terribly limited. I couldn't make my sympathies go round two million people; I should be wretched" (28).

Sympathy, in a general sense, means an understanding and sharing of the feeling of another or others. It often suggests a feeling of compassion or commiseration.[2] Mrs. March's remarks sound unusual because sympathy is presented as a special form of asset which the owner, once confronted with misery and poverty, has to dispense in order to comfort herself and ameliorate the situation. Since this asset, like other properties, has its limitation in quantity, its dispensation becomes simultaneously an economic issue (i.e., the well-calculated expense of sympathy) and a moral one (i.e., the sharing of misfortune with society).

A judicious and an economical utilization of sympathy is not just an insignificant private concern of the Marches. It was, in fact, a major public concern in the nineteenth century when competition was strongly advocated and self-interest encouraged. Howells was also deeply concerned with this issue of sympathy during the time he was writing the novel. His deep concern is traceable in his realistic depiction of the socioeconomic life of the day and in the utopian conclusion of the novel.

Over a century before, sympathy, particularly its relation to capitalist economy, had attracted the attention of Adam Smith, the famous eighteenth-century economist. *The Theory of Moral Sentiments* (1759), Smith's first work, was a study of moral philosophy with a focus on the influence of sympathy. In his definition of sympathy, Smith states, "The word sympathy, in its most proper and primitive signification, denotes our fellow-feeling with the sufferings, not that with the enjoyments, of others."[3] Smith begins his book by stating that all human beings, virtuous or ruffian, are capable of experiencing such sentiments as pity, compassion, or sorrow. But Smith clearly uses the word to mean "compassion" and "commiseration."[4] By our imagination, Smith says, we place ourselves in another person's situation, conceive ourselves enduring the same sufferings as he does, and thus form some idea of his sensations as well as an understanding of his situation.[5] The sentiments that we experience upon the sight of the sufferer may not be identical with those of the sufferer; however, this process of imaginative transposition and identification, or sympathy, undoubtedly brings the spectator and the object closer.

To be sympathetic is to be socially involved since the sympathizer brings the other person's situation into his or imaginatively experiences the situation of the sufferer. Showing sympathy also carries a moral implication, a point that Smith confirms in his emotional statement, "How amiable does he appear to be, whose sympathetic heart seems to re-echo all the sentiments of those with whom he converses, who grieves for their calamities, who resents their injuries, and who rejoices at their good fortune!"[6] With his sympathetic act, such an affectionate friend can infuse consolation in the heart of the sufferer. On the other hand, an unsympathetic person, insensible to the happiness or misery of other people, is "disagreeable" as his presence can only give "pain" to everyone with whom he has contact. For this very reason, Smith makes an unequivocal conclusion that sympathy "cannot, in any sense, be regarded as a selfish principle."[7]

Two decades later, however, this moral advocate of sympathy gave a surprisingly contrasting picture of the *homo economicus*, or the economic man of the modern world, in *The Wealth of Nations* (1776). Self-interest is stressed as a virtuous motive with which individuals promote social good.[8] Emphasizing the interdependence of human beings, Smith points out that, though man constantly seeks help from his brethren, it is in vain to expect the help merely from their benevolence. Benevolence, used as synonymous with "sympathy," comes with and is propagated by self-interest. "Give me that which I want, and you shall have this which you want, is the meaning of every such offer."[9] In other words, no help will be offered unless the donor perceives a potential return or profit. Hence comes Smith's famous statement:

> It is not from the benevolence of the butcher, the brewer, or the baker, that we expect our dinner, but from their regard to their own interest. We address ourselves, not to their humanity but to their self-love, and never talk to them of our own necessities but of their advantages.[10]

Self-interest, Smith claims, is the prime psychological drive in man as an economic being. In any economy which is based on exchange, it is self-interest rather than benevolence that operates. Smith further defends this by arguing that the individual strivings for self-interest would add up to the social good.[11] Pursuing one's own interest may unintentionally promote that of the society "more effectually." In fact, Smith concludes, "I have never known much good done by those who affected to trade for the public good."[12]

The change in Adam Smith's view from claiming sympathy as a moral and virtuous attribute to hailing self-interest as a basic force in socioeconomic progression, is astounding. Smith has clearly switched his standpoint from a call for sympathy as a social bond to a confirmation of the significance of self-interest in social and economic life. In *The Wealth of the Nations*, Smith still employs such terms as "benevolence" and "humanity" as mentioned above, but the term "benevolence" carries, at most, the partial meaning of "sympathy," that is, entering into the feelings of another. It differs from compassion, commiseration, or brother-feeling. Self-interest and sympathy are mutually exclusive. Self-interest may invoke a feeling of others, but it simultaneously deters one from being compassionate.

America in the 1880s saw a development of widespread social theories, many of which addressed this issue of "sympathy" and regarded it as both an economic and a moral issue. Henry George, for example, contended that "self-interest," which arose from economic scarcity, was "unnatural." He focused his attention on material problems and suggested that "self-interest" was caused by insecurity, a pervasive and increasingly difficult problem in human life. George believed that, once we were able to banish economic scarcity, an abundant fellow love would emerge.[13]

The Danish-American socialist Lawrence Gronlund's *The Cooperative Commonwealth* (1884), a book that exerted enormous influence on Howells,[14] labels the issue of "sympathy" as "the crown of morals."[15] Like Adam Smith in *The Theory of Moral Sentiments*, Gronlund stresses that sympathy is "fellow-feeling" and compassion. "To sympathize is to make the pleasure and pain of our fellows our own." However, Gronlund points out that sympathy grows "but little" because "suffering is daily inflicted or daily displayed by associates."[16] Gronlund thus differentiates his point from Smith's in *The Wealth of the Nation* as he stresses the fact that suffering, aggravated by a competitive economy of self-interest, suffocates the growth of sympathy. Sympathy and self-interest, to Gronlund, are incompatible.

Gronlund delineates the social and economic system of America, which, as he observes, has widened the gap between the rich and the poor, and breeds inequality among social classes. The difference between Gronlund's and Smith's views is further underlined with Gronlund's criticism of the "cut-throat competition," which has been praised as a wonderful mechanism in accumulation and economic development by advocates of the "gospel of wealth." Gronlund calls "competition" a "very slippery word" since it advances only the successful at the cost of others, which possibly constitute the majority.[17] Gronlund shows the wage worker's condition as "servitude in substance and form."[18] He condemns the capitalist system as "vicious and morally injurious" since a master-servant or master-slave relationship exists in both social and domestic spheres.

Sympathy, a moral sentiment, is shown to be economically based. While Smith praises self-interest as a virtuous motive, Gronlund believes that individualism, "the moving power" of the industrial system, "stifles all sympathetic sentiments."[19] Individualism incites men to pursue their own success and happiness, with complete indifference to other people. To make social improvements, by eradicating individualism and by cultivating a sympathetic relation among people, a fundamental change is required of economic relations, which are "the foundation of even the highest form of morals."[20] Sympathy suggests and breeds equality. It differs from pity "which indicates a posture of superiority to the object."[21] Showing sympathy is a democratic gesture, harmonizing social, political and economical differences. The necessary condition of sympathy is found in Gronlund's blueprint of a commonwealth: "*substantial*, perhaps absolute, *equality*."[22] This socially as well as economically equal relation will be "a moral—a sympathetic relation." Everyone is an equal member of the family, and no one will be so slavish as to subject oneself to any disreputable position.

Gronlund's book was succeeded a few years later by Edward Bellamy's best selling *Looking Backward* in 1888,[23] when Howells was working on his *A Hazard of New Fortunes*. *Looking Backward* introduces to us a wonderful new society structured on "the basis of equality" by its first-person narrator Julian West, a nineteenth-century wealthy Bostonian, who is hypnotized to sleep in the cellar vault of his house and awakened by Dr. Leete in the year of 2000.

By contrasting the twenty-first century Utopian society with the nineteenth-century Boston, Bellamy demonstrates that sympathy and the lack of sympathy are features that distinguish the two. The nineteenth-century society is compared to "a prodigious coach" that the masses drag toilsomely along a steep and sandy road. Despite the difficulty of drawing the coach along, the passengers enjoy the breeze on the top and never get down even at the steepest ascent. They "enjoy the scenery at their leisure, or critically discuss the merits of the straining team."[24]

> For all that they were so easy, the seats were very insecure, and at every sudden jolt of the coach persons were slipping out of them and falling to the ground, where they were instantly compelled to take hold of the rope and help to drag the coach on which they had before ridden so pleasantly. It was naturally regarded as a terrible misfortune to lose one's seat, and the apprehension that this might happen to them or their friends was a constant cloud upon the happiness of those who rode.[25]

Bellamy stresses that in the nineteenth century, when one's fortune is built on other people's misfortunes, cut-throat competition formulates one's unsympathetic viewpoint and determines one's behavior. It is an age of individualism when people of Boston put up three hundred thousand umbrellas over themselves and their wives, and give their neighbors the drippings.[26] In the twenty-first century, however, one enormous umbrella is used to protect the whole society. "Looking Forward," Bellamy's article in the first issue of *The Nationalist* in 1889, explicates the Nationalist movement by listing its four characteristics, which, Bellamy believes, will guarantee the "ultimate triumph." Among these four characteristics, "unselfishness" stands as the first. Bellamy sees fellow-feeling, which is "the animating principle of Nationalism," as "a religion in itself." He sees the principle of fraternal co-operation as both "the only true science of wealth-production" and "the only moral basis for society." The latter is a consideration so much more important that it would be attained even with the price of sacrificing wealth.[27]

Both Gronlund and Bellamy were major influences on Howells's thinking in the late 1880s.[28] To Howells, Gronlund's book was a prophecy of a new society based on "the broad principle that those who do not work shall not eat, and that no man who is willing to work shall starve."[29] Howells, who detested the ferocious competition in urban capitalism, believed that selfishness could only lead to destruction, and capitalism produced "inequalities" which prevented "the brotherhood." The influences of his Swedenborgian father and Tolstoyan Christian socialism found an echo in Gronlund's and Bellamy's works, which called for sympathy among people regardless of social background.

Nevertheless, the most significant influence in this respect on Howells and the writing of this novel was the Haymarket event on May 4, 1886, when a bomb was thrown in at a peaceful gathering organized by anarchists in Chicago. Seven policemen were killed and many civilians severely wounded. A few years earlier, "the smiling aspect" of life, Howells's optimistic view, had already begun to be shadowed by a tragic tone that Miss Kingsbury expresses at the dinner party in Mr. Corey's house in *The Rise of Silas Lapham*: "I have often thought of our great, cool houses standing useless here, and the thousands of poor creatures stifling in their holes and dens, and the little children dying for wholesome shelter. How cruelly selfish we are!"[30] And this view became even darker after the Haymarket event and the subsequent trial of eight anarchists between 1886 and 1888 when Howells, who endeavored to set them free, was confronted with a relentless and unsympathetic populace and legislature.

Immediately after the Haymarket explosion, the city of Chicago was seized with fear, hatred, and panic. People gathered on street corners talking about the event. Newspapers, magazines, and even clergymen in Sunday sermons made sensational and passionate denunciation of the "Bloody Brutes," "Red Ruffians," "Bomb Throwers," and "Fiends." The impression was created that Albert Parson, the leading German socialist arrested, and his friends had thrown the murdering bomb. Since most of the anarchists were German immigrants, the public identified anarchism with foreigners and subversion. The Haymarket explosion raised xenophobia to an unprecedented intense level.[31] And a fear of subversion triggered "a campaign of radical-baiting rarely if ever surpassed" in American history. The explosion brought on "the first major 'Red Scare'" in America.[32] For weeks and months, the public showed a fiery indignation against anarchists, the radical movement, and anyone who had "ever expressed the faintest sympathy with it."[33] Even the Knights of Labor, a labor organization, quickly dissociated itself from the anarchists by stating that no "sympathy" would be given to "the band of cowardly murderers, cut-throats and robbers."[34]

On August 20, 1887, the jury's verdict was read that all the eight anarchists on trial were found "guilty of murder" and seven of them were sentenced to death. The verdict was applauded by an overwhelming majority across the nation, rejoicing that "law and order had triumphed over anarchy and subversion."[35] Any doubt, even the slightest one, in the validity of the trial, the verdict, or the sentences, would be construed as "a token of anarchist sympathies." The necessity of establishing a solid judicial case, proving beyond reasonable doubt that these accused were actually involved in throwing the bomb, was dismissed as "reflecting sympathy for the elements that threatened the safety and well-being of the city."[36]

Howells, America's leading man of letters, was deeply affected by this event, which was always in his "waking thoughts" for many months. He wrote to a friend, ". . . it is the last thing when I lie down, and the first thing when I rise up; it blackens my life."[37] In his letter to George William Curtis, editor of *Harper's Weekly*, Howells expressed his concern for the defendants and "the calamity which error in it must embody." He felt that the defendants were victimized and "doomed to suffer for their opinions' sake" by the trial proceedings which were "hysterical and unjust."[38] He demonstrated his deep sympathy toward these anarchists, whom he believed innocent, and he publicly allied himself with the cause of clemency for them. On September 25, Howells wrote a letter to Judge Roger A. Pryor, who was to serve as counsel for the anarchists on their appeal to the Supreme Court. In his letter, Howells stated, "I have never believed them guilty of murder, or of anything but their opinions, and I do not think they were justly convicted."[39] As soon as the appeal was turned down, Howells surprised the public by having a letter published in the influential *New York Tribune*, stating his attempt to persuade the Governor of Illinois "to commute the death penalty of the Anarchists to imprisonment."[40]

> But the worst is still for a very few days reparable; the men sentenced to death are still alive, and their lives may be finally saved through the clemency of the Governor, whose prerogative is now the supreme law in their case. I conjure all those who believe that it would be either injustice or impolicy to put them to death, to join in urging him by petition, by letter, through the press, and from the pulpit and the platform, to use his power, in the only direction where power can never be misused, for the mitigation of their punishment.[41]

It was the "clemency"—compassionate feelings or sympathy—of the governor as well as the public that Howells was trying to seek by publicizing this letter to the editor. Having failed in his great effort to win support from well-known writers such as George W. Curtis and John Greenleaf Whittier, Howells had to fight alone and to sustain "the coast-to-coast abuse" as a result of "his lonely act of courage."[42] He was castigated in newspapers throughout the country, some of which, he remarked, "abused me as heartily as if I had proclaimed myself a dynamiter."[43] Instead of winning public sympathy for the anarchists, Howells only isolated himself. An editor in Maine, for example, denounced him indignantly, "The position which you have taken, Mr. Howells, must sever you from the loyal friendship of thousands of your readers and admirers."[44]

Nevertheless, Howells insisted on showing sympathy with the anarchists. On November 12, the day after four of the anarchists were hanged, the New York *Sun* put a headline "Honoring the Anarchists," under which was an article describing a Boston meeting attended by "a crowd that howled derisively in response to the scathing denunciation of the Government by the speakers." The article reported that the hall was "lined with blood-red cloth," and "W. D. Howells, the author, sent a letter sympathizing with the Anarchist movement." The following day, H. M. Alden, the editor of *Harper*'s, requested that Howells publicly disown the alleged expression of sympathy.[45] A few days later, Howells, in his letter to his sister, Annie, mentioned sympathy again: "Elinor [Howells's wife] and I both no longer care for the world's life, and would like to be settled somewhere very humbly and simply, where we would be socially identified with the principles of progress and sympathy for the struggling mass."[46]

All these, taken together, indicate that, either to Howells or to the public, sympathy with these social revolutionaries was seriously regarded as a social and economic issue.[47] How could anarchists win public sympathy? How could the expression of sympathy be voiced, circulated, recognized and accepted? And how could Howells himself win public sympathy? In the same letter to Annie, Howells wrote that he could not write about the anarchists, but he would find way to "do justice to these irreparably wronged men" sometime in the future.[48] And his wish was probably fulfilled by his writing of *Annie Kilburn* (1888) and *Hazard*.

Annie Kilburn, the novel that precedes *Hazard*, is concerned with an attempt to establish a social union, a scheme that is meant to bring together all social classes—particularly workers and their benefactors—at Hatboro, Massachusetts.[49] Annie Kilburn, a native of the town, comes back from Rome and voluntarily carries on this task. Nevertheless, her passion is soon extinguished by the cruel reality: tension increased by the fund-raising, ineffectiveness of the money in creating new ties, and the snobbery and social irrelevance of the rich families. Eventually, she changes her views. She accepts and even defends Rev. Julius W. Peck's argument that "good is from the heart" and "money can't buy a true sympathy between rich and poor."

The "utter failure" of Kilburn's experiment brings out the issue of sympathy that Peck as well as Howells attempts to propose. Answering Kilburn's doubt about the power of money early in the novel, Peck says,

> "Money is a palliative, but it can't cure. It can sometimes create a bond of gratitude perhaps, but it can't create sympathy between rich and poor."
>
> "But *why* can't it?"
>
> "Because sympathy—common feeling—the sense of fraternity—can spring only from like experiences, like hopes, like fears. And money can't buy these."[50]

Sympathy suggests equality and commonality. It originates from "an impulse of love," and it is to be offered by someone as "a brother of those who need it," not as "a patron."[51] But the wealthy meet the poor only "in the odious character of a patron."[52] Like Kilburn, Peck is also "interested to see the experiment of bringing the different grades of society together." But he is opposed to the scheme because he has perceived that it is not enough to rely upon "money," and that Kilburn's experiment is destined to be futile in the present socioeconomic condition with class division and social inequality.[53]

The failure, complicated by Peck's tragic death, is commented on by Dr. Morrell, a jeering bystander:

> "We people of leisure, or comparative leisure, have really nothing in common with you people who work with your hands for a living; and as we really can't be friends with you, we won't patronize you. We won't advise you, and we won't help you; but here's the money. If you fail, you fail; and if you succeed, you won't succeed by our aid and comfort."[54]

Dr. Morrell's remarks here deride Kilburn's futile efforts to create a tie of sympathy and suggest that socioeconomic inequality is absolute and unavoidable. But his remarks help to raise the very issue that Howells wanted the society to re-examine. Howells ended the novel with a failure, but his own endeavor to create a tie of sympathy among all social classes continued. It was the very issue that preoccupied Howells during the turbulent late 1880s. And this same issue became the major concern of his next novel *Hazard.*

The house-hunting section at the beginning of *Hazard* has often been criticized for being disproportionately large, though the novel clearly marks the peak of Howells's literary achievement in its moral, aesthetic, and social aspects.[55] Even Howells himself apologized that this section incorporated "long stretches of carpentry where I arrived at little or nothing of the real edifice."[56] But when this "unwieldy" first section is read against the major theme of sympathy, it seems fitting and appropriate. The house-hunting section brings the reader's attention to the forgotten interiors of the city. It is a necessary introduction of the milieu and a comprehensive prelude to the call for sympathy as well as social reform.

The house-hunting experience teaches the Marches that an invisible line, like the one dividing East and West in New York City, resolutely separates the rich from the poor. During their visit to Jacob Dryfoos's house, the Marches have a brief conversation with Mrs. Mandel about the weather in New York. Mrs. Mandel warns these two Bostonians of the malicious effect of the weather there.

> "Oh, I'm sure they can't be worse than *our* winds," Mrs. Mandel returned, caressingly.
>
> "If we escape New York pneumonia," March laughed, "it will be only to fall a prey to New York malaria as soon as the frost is out of the ground."
>
> "Oh, but you know," said Mrs. Mandel, "I think our malaria has really been slandered a little. It's more a matter of drainage—of plumbing. I don't believe it would be possible for malaria to get into *this* house, we've had it gone over so thoroughly." (152-53)

Superficially, it sounds like a light conversation, discussing weather and the misconceived nature of malaria. And Mr. March's amusing comment at this juncture appears merely reaffirming the problem of the epidemic:

> "If Mrs. March could have had her way, we should have had the drainage of our whole ward put in order," said her husband, "before we ventured to take a furnished apartment for the winter." (153)

March means that his wife, with her wide sympathy, would disseminate her compassion and eliminate the social problem for the whole community. However, the word "ward," which may also mean a room or a division in a hospital, overshadows the amusing tone of March's comment with the serious implication that the region is epidemic-infested.

The invisible line that protects the rich from being infected by the epidemic, keeps them away from the suffering of the poor. The epidemic as a metaphor of poverty has been employed earlier when the Marches stroll along poverty-stricken slum areas.

> It was not the abode of the extremest poverty, but of a poverty as hopeless as any in the world, transmitting itself from generation to generation, and establishing conditions of permanency to which human life adjusts itself as it does to those of some incurable disease, like leprosy. (65)

The diseases mentioned, malaria and leprosy, are more than transmittable epidemics in the text here. They are really social diseases that, along with the "hopeless" poverty, pass from one generation to another. Truly, as epidemics, they are transmittable; yet as social diseases, they seem not transmittable because they can never infect the rich, who are separated and protected behind the heavy walls of their mansions. The line that circumscribes poverty ruthlessly confines these diseases. Mrs. Mandel's confidence in immunity and her emphatic "*this* house" clearly indicate a form of privileged aloofness from a social disease that harasses the rest of the community.

The house hunting experience shows the Marches that there is no mutual exchange of fellow feelings or sympathy between the rich and the poor. Dryfoos's "indistinctive brownstone house" is "delicately decorated in white and gold, and furnished with a sort of extravagant good taste." The material extravagance suggests the awesome potency and supremacy of the host. "[E]verything in the room meant money too plainly, and too much of it" (151).

While superiority in material possession seems to endow the rich, such as the Dryfooses, with freedom to choose and to show themselves, it insulates them from the poor who have to take whatever they get and whose shabby apartments won't give "any conception of home." The rich are aloof from even the sight of the dirty, noisy, poor neighborhood. In fact, the insulation is so complete that the Dryfooses have not received even a single call from their neighbor for three years (154).

Roaming through New York on foot and by coupe, the Marches get acquainted with the city, and this acquaintance is a form of education, provoking sympathy in the Marches. When the couple sit on the coupe with the window down, travelling through a tenement-house street, they are content with a detached aesthetic appreciation of the picturesqueness of the street. As soon as Mrs. March pulls up her window of the coupe, they are confronted with the reality of the "disgusting street," and their esthetic contentment instantly evaporates (65). But the sight evokes some thoughts in Basil: ". . . I wonder what they think of us, making this gorgeous progress through their midst? I suppose they think we're rich, and hate us—if they hate rich people; they don't look as if they hated anybody" (65). Basil's "monologue" indicates that the street has evoked an imaginative emotional transposition in his mind. He starts to conceive what the thought is of those people who "spend their whole lives in it . . . with no hopes of driving out of it, except in a hearse" (65). The scene surely brings about a recognition of March's own "humane sentiments." He reproaches his wife who is extraordinarily picky in her choice of the apartment. "Doesn't it make you feel rather small and otherwise unworthy when you see the kind of street these fellow-beings of yours live in, and then think how particular you are about locality and the number of bell-pulls?" (66).

The house-hunting section thus illustrates the relationship between sympathy and the knowledge of the object being observed. Close contact and close observation produce sound knowledge to be followed by sympathetic feelings, which simultaneously welcome further knowledge. In other words, sympathy and knowledge come together. The walk on Broadway and Washington Square, and the sight of the faces of different ethnic backgrounds remind the Marches of "the familiar picturesque raggedness of southern Europe." Then March sits down to get a shine on his boots.

> March thought he sufficiently expressed his tacit sympathy in sitting down on one of the iron benches with his wife, and letting a little Neapolitan put a superfluous shine on his boots, while their desultory comment wandered with equal esteem to the old-fashioned American respectability which keeps the north side of the square in vast mansions of red brick, and the international shabbiness which has invaded the southern border, and broken it up into lodging-houses, shops, beer-gardens, and studios. (55-56)

This lengthy and winding sentence does not give a clear and direct description as to how March expresses his sympathy. It is hardly distinguishable whether March has expressed his "tacit sympathy" merely by having the "little Neapolitan" shine his boots or by both making comments on the contrasts in the area and having his boots shined. But the momentary pause certainly gives March a chance to make "desultory comment with equal esteem" on class divisions, diverse racial components, and intense socioeconomic conflicts. The phrase "equal esteem" suggests both knowledge and sympathy. Observing the city is both an act of showing sympathy, and a way to generate and reinforce sympathy.

Howells stresses the importance of direct involvement in relation to sympathy by illustrating that neither a fleeting nor an indirect contact will bring a sympathetic understanding or evoke sympathetic feelings in the observer. The newly constructed elevated railroad that sweeps across the city above the threatening crowd externalizes the otherwise inaccessible second- and third-floor interiors to the passenger: a family party of work-folks at late tea, a solitary sewing woman, a mother fondling her baby, a sleeping man and a young couple in love. But the serenity, security, and exclusiveness, characteristics of a good society, suggested by the scene, only distance the viewer from the cruel reality of poverty and try to convince him that "there is no misery."[57] As March has commented earlier, "Those bends in the L . . . they're the gayest things in the world. Perfectly atrocious, of course, but incomparably picturesque! . . . New York may be splendidly gay or squalidly gay, but, prince or pauper, it's gay always" (62). The obsessive repetition of the word "gay" exposes and expands the distance between the effect of the "L" and the reality that the "L" has hidden. The magnificent sight of the night trains on the tracks is an awesome spectacle, but the trains will not help to produce any knowledge or sympathy since they are "tractable, reckless, will-less—organized lifelessness full of a strange semblance of life" (77). The passengers on these "fabled monsters of Arab story" will never be able to get a sympathetic feeling for others since they do not even have a control of themselves.

If the house hunting section provides an introduction of the existent class division and the socioeconomic milieu, the establishment of *Every Other Week* may be seen as an effort to build mutual understandings and curb the competition as well as conduct a successful literary magazine. The word "mutual" is a fitting description of *Every Other Week*, a literary magazine that March and Fulkerson prepare to establish. When selecting the title for the magazine, March suggests *The Round Robin*, which, as he explains, expresses "the central idea of irresponsibility" and is exactly the principle of the magazine: "everybody is to share the profits and be exempt from the losses" (10). And the notion of common-feelings and mutual connection is reinforced by some other suggested titles, such as *The Mutual* and *From Sea to Sea*.

However, what distinguishes this literary project is the emphasis on the exchange of sympathy as an asset, an unusual concept that echoes Mrs. March's remarks mentioned earlier. The magazine is a capitalist enterprise in which Dryfoos supplies and controls the capital while Fulkerson manages the business, and contributors and editors provide labor. But sympathy is shown to be an essential monetary unit for exchange or calculation of the profit. Fulkerson solicits March not for editorial experience but for his broad "sympathies" (9). His "sympathies" become the asset that he has to contribute to ensure the success of the magazine. And the public sympathy is recognized and calculated as the profit—or an unignorable part of the profit—for the magazine. The success of this literary enterprise is contingent upon the magazine's appeal to women readers and its capacity in arousing public "curiosity" or "public sympathy" (18). Fulkerson hopes that the novelty of the literary enterprise can "pique curiosity" and even arouse "public sympathy" (18).

With Angus Beaton, Berthold Lindau, Colonel Woodburn, Margaret Vance and Conrad Dryfoos, Howells presents four different types of characters whose different degrees of sympathy are unfolded through their views of class division, inequality, and human relationships. Angus Beaton, a talented but irresponsible artist, appears to be an eccentric with an "elusive, facile, adaptable, unpractical" nature (119). The buildings that he designs can be "very striking, very original, very *chic*, very everything but habitable" (119). He criticizes the idea that sculpture is accessory to architecture, and he believes that it ought to be "the other way:" "temples should be raised to enshrine statues, not statues made to ornament temples" (119). He despises commercialization and accuses the rich patrons of being uninterested in art. Yet he can never sever himself from the marketplace as he is never willing to give up supplying the syndicate letters to Fulkerson for ten dollars a week.

Beaton's eccentricity is a special form of selfishness. While following his own whim, Beaton shows no concern with other people's feelings, emotions, or interests. Howells writes,

> [H]e neglected everybody, and only remembered them when it suited his whim or his convenience; but he fiercely resented the inattention of others toward himself. He had no scruple about breaking an engagement or failing to keep an appointment; he made promises without thinking of their fulfilment. . . . (128)

Coming from the country, he finds that New York City provides some potential opportunities for his success. And he looks for those chances which might help to sell his artistic talent. It is not long before he has almost completely forgotten Alma Leighton and her mother, who used to provide him with board before he came to New York. Upon Wetmore's comment on Alma Leighton, Beaton yields to "the threefold impulse of conscience, of curiosity, of inclination" and decides to visit the family, who have also come to New York (130). Yet none of these multiple motivations is truly sympathetic. Beaton seems forever hesitant. He is calculating and unwilling to give his compassion and love to Alma because of the Leightons' insecure economic situation, though he is deeply attracted by Alma's beauty, talent and refinement (235, 276, 365, 403). The "intangible obligations of mutual kindness" between him and the Leightons thus hang loosely upon him. For the sake of his own "convenience," he could break from the Leightons at any moment, and it would not hurt him at all (242-43).

Beaton is not what Fulkerson calls one with "the most subtle and refined sympathies" (141). Instead he is a man who covets other people's sympathy (468). He is eager to receive other people's compassion; yet he shows no respect toward the feelings of others. Fulkerson's description is true only in the sense that Beaton habitually transfers his position to another party's in his imagination, the "swift internal dramatization" which constantly goes on in his mind (135). Yet his "sympathy" never goes a step further (172, 456). He does not want to reach out to marry or help Alma, who is in need of financial assistance. He is satisfied with constructing in his mind a "common future" in which their lives and work are "united" (243). On very rare occasions, the feeling of sympathy does seem to strike Beaton, yet it is merely momentary and inevitably suppressed by his own selfishness. For a certain period of time, Beaton is often in the "martyr mood" and wishes to help his poor father, who is in desperate need of money. He decides not to purchase Chianti and an overcoat for himself so that he will have money to pay off his father's debt. Nevertheless, his plan is aborted and the moment of sympathetic "actual sacrifice" is postponed, because he purchases the overcoat in "an anguish of self-reproach" (382).

Lindau, a character evidently based on the Haymarket anarchist victims, forms a sharp contrast to Beaton. If Beaton is the type that stands for selfishness in the novel, Lindau is one for sympathy. With a passionate nature, Lindau has an inclination for such Romantic poets as Goethe and Heine. From Germany he came to America and voluntarily participated in the Civil War, in which he lost one arm. This "gentle" and "generous" soul ends up poor and homeless. Nevertheless, he is happy to identify himself with the poor. Even living in Greenwich Village makes him feel "a lidtle too moch of an aristograt." He moves into the slum area so that he can see the poor all the time and will never forget them. His sympathetic attachment to the poor enables him to comprehend and enjoy the "lidtle tricks" of the children in the neighborhood, and he speaks fondly of these poor brothers. "We onderstand each other," as he claims (190). He joyfully considers himself as part of the group, and he is clearly accepted as a member of the community.

Lindau's existence constitutes a serious criticism of the economic system, and his heterogeneity in accent, ethnicity, and ideology highlights the otherness suppressed and marginalized by society. Lindau believes that millionaires are all guilty of stealing money. He thinks that it is possible to earn a few thousand honest dollars a year, but no honest man—a worker, poet, or artist—can ever become a millionaire through work. The "oppressors" or "tyrants" "make the millions" by giving toils to their helpless brothers and allowing them "to earn enough to keep life in them" (191). He reproaches American democracy "as a shuffling evasion" and tells Mrs. March that there is no equality in this democratic country. The poor do not share an equal stand before the law or in their pursuit of happiness.

At the same time, Lindau, with his highly idealistic and fanatical views, alienates himself from society. Lindau's radical views are often impractical. He strives quixotically to free himself from being a slave of money and to detach himself from the existent marketplace. He used to teach March German for free as he refused to be engaged in monetary exchange. His question to March, "How much money can a man honestly earn without wronging or oppressing some other man?" further illustrates the absurdity of his theory and its impracticability, since one can never transcend the economic system and live like a Robinson Crusoe. Guided by his radical theory, Lindau deliberately chooses March's apartment, instead of going to the editorial office, for his business transaction with the magazine. For his own writing, Lindau demands immediate payment in cash rather than in check because he believes that a check suggests the banking system and "the capitalistic manipulation of the people's money." Moreover, he wants to receive his "honestly earned" money only from March's hand (317). Nevertheless, from the day he starts to work for the magazine, Lindau unknowingly becomes a part of the corporation that he condemns, and begins to share the increase of Dryfoos's capital. Later, as he realizes that it is Dryfoos's money "*mate* by sbeculation," Lindau returns the pay and triumphantly declares that "I am a free man," a statement which is quixotical in nature (318-19, 363).

Lindau's condemnatory judgment of all the rich and his philosophy of violence concerning the whole political and economic system repel even his admirers and potential supporters. Mrs. March, for example, intends to show her sympathy toward his integrity, dedication, and suffering. His unreserved "rebellious mind," however, outlaws him from her "sympathy" when Mrs. March feels that he is detestable instead (292-93, 451). To both March and his wife, Lindau, committed to violence and willfulness, may cause even "greater wrong" in his fight against injustice and disorder (451).

Likewise, Colonel Woodburn, a Southern gentleman, criticizes capitalist economy and commercialization. Woodburn acknowledges that the South, under the influence of the North, is "advancing with enormous strides," but in the direction of commercialism (172). To Woodburn, commercialism is the "virus" or poison which has destroyed the South's "divine institution" and isolated those whose interests are "in another direction" (172, 337). The spirit of commercialism, Woodburn believes, despises and repels traditional virtues, such as generosity, delicacy, chivalry and honesty. Throughout the nation, people fervidly pursue money and try to establish their prosperity on others' adversity. The dollar has become "the measure of every value" and "the stamp of every success," and it has become "the final reward" of everything, even including art (174).

Capitalist economy and commercialization, Woodburn believes, have led to competition and animosity among human beings. The "infernal impulse of competition" have brought "a perpetual warfare" and forced everyone to trick, betray, and destroy one another in order to gain success and money (337). He is concerned with the future of the country. Tracing the history of this country, which began as a simple, agricultural society, Woodburn shows that commercialism has brought nearly incalculable damage to this remarkable new nation: competition is the agency that has destroyed thousands of small businesses, and much of the industry is under the domination of ruthless monopolies. He is worried that the nation might soon be dominated by a few tycoons (337-38).

Even though Woodburn's criticism of capitalism wins Lindau's consent, Woodburn's beliefs are essentially different from Lindau's. Woodburn has never meant to establish a society which breeds and welcomes brotherly feelings; he only aims to revive the slavery system and proclaims that a universal benevolent slavery should be the only solution to the labor problem. He proposes to construct an ideal new society, built upon the idea of "responsibility."

> The enlightened, the moneyed, the recultivated class shall be responsible to the central authority—emperor, duke, president; the name does not matter—for the national expense and the national defence, and it shall be responsible to the working classes of all kinds for homes and lands and implements, and the opportunity to labor at all times. The working classes shall be responsible to the leisure class for the support of its dignity in peace, and shall be subject to its command in war. The rich shall warrant the poor against planless production and the ruin that now follows, against danger from without and famine from within, and the poor—" (344)

In such a revised slavery system, Woodburn claims, the laborers would be "insured" and "protected" (179). It is such an ideal condition that there will be no competition, treachery, fraud, or terror.

Woodburn's rhetoric resonates the pro-slavery eulogy in the Old South. The defenders of Southern slavery used to argue that slavery system was better than capitalist system partly because there were no competition and hazards. Much of the competition among the laborers was said to have originated from the free labor system. The laborers had to compete against each other for available work in order to get the means of subsistence.[58] Slavery system was regarded as a "protection from pauperism."[59] James Henley Thornwell, a Presbyterian expounder of pro-slavery theory, argued that "slavery is nothing but an organization of labor, and an organization by virtue of which labor and capital are made to coincide."[60] Since the labor was capital, many conflicts, including that of interest between employees and the employer, would lose their foundations in slavery system. The master would take good care of the slave, and there would be no anxieties from want, mistreatment, or disability. George Fitzhugh, a pro-slavery supporter of Virginia, even remarked that "every Southern slave has an estate in tail, indefeasible by fine and recovery, in the lands of the South. If his present master cannot support him, he must sell him to one who can."[61]

Woodburn proposes to substitute the protective "responsibility" of the money class for sympathy. His ideal system, in which class divisions still exist and the rich dominate the poor, is a revised slavery system, an even stricter and more oppressive form of social and economic structure (343-44). For this reason, it is understandable why Woodburn rarely discusses or even mentions sympathy. His sympathy, if it does exist, is conditional and limited to the bygone aristocrat and the landed gentry. In the slavery system, there can be no sympathy between the master and the slave or among the slaves because slaves are properties, possessed by slaveholders. They are denied civil rights and freedom, and they are forced to perform compulsory labor. What the slave can expect from the master in Woodburn's system is not sympathy but mercy, not compassion out of the humanitarian concern but care in order to preserve the value of the property.

Conrad Dryfoos and Margaret Vance in the novel stand out as a couple of incredibly pure human creatures. Conrad is a saint, and he does not have "the stain of a base thought" (280). Like Lindau, Conrad is wholeheartedly sympathetic with the poor. He prefers the rigors of charity work among the poor to the luxurious lifestyle of his class. He is willing to give the poor folks not only his money but also his time, knowledge, love, and even his life. And he strives to cultivate sympathetic feelings in society. Unlike Lindau, to whom only violence is conducive to a social change for equality, Conrad believes that a mutual understanding between the rich and the poor will bring harmony and peace to society. He feels that "the only trouble is that we don't know one another well enough" (147). Against his father's will, he studies to be a preacher, to awaken the conscience of the rich and to bring about social change. He values highly March's sketches of New York, and he encourages him to publish these sketches in the magazine to make "the comfortable people understand how the uncomfortable people live" (147).

Margaret is prolific in sympathies, which are "intellectual rather than sentimental" (247). At the reception at Mrs. Horn's house, Margaret plays a key role in uniting the fashionable people and the esthetic people "on common ground" (243). Mrs. Horn's house is a literary house with "artistic qualifications," where writers and artists frequently gather and enjoy free exchange of their ideas (243). It seems like the only house in New York which offers such a utopian oasis in a commercialized world. The "esthetic sympathies" of the hostess help to generate a democratic yet intellectual sphere which counteracts the negative effect of commercialism:

> There was great ease there, and simplicity; and if there was not distinction, it was not for want of distinguished people, but because there seems to be some solvent in New York life that reduces all men to a common level, that touches everybody with its potent magic and brings to the surface the deeply underlying nobody. (243)

While Beaton deplores that the atmosphere of "the salon," if it can be thus named, is vulgar and disorderly, Margaret argues that such "plebeian" and democratic exchanges should be more preferable to writers and artists. This social place is indiscriminating, intellectually delightful, and pleasing. Here equality and mutual communications are conditioned upon an awakening of "some temperaments" and "consciousness," and "egotism" (243-44).

Margaret shows no hesitation in giving sympathy to the socially destitute, such as the Dryfooses, who need as much philanthropy as the financially destitute. She repudiates the commercialism of society, where an unselfish act becomes impossible and all favors mean to be "really bargains" (254). She discusses with Mrs. Horn her plan to visit Dryfoos's daughters, and Mrs. Horn's response is a reminder of Adam Smith. To do an unselfish act, Mrs. Horn says, is "quixotic." "Society doesn't rest upon any such basis. It can't; it would go to pieces, if people acted from unselfish motives" (253-54). Despite Mrs. Horn's admonition, Margaret refuses to transform her own sympathy into a gift for exchange, and she goes to visit Alma and Christine Dryfoos simply to "do them a pleasure" and "make them happy"[62] (254-59).

Conrad and Margaret constitute a complementary whole in cultivating sympathetic feelings in society. Being altruistic and devoted to the financially destitute, Conrad has somehow neglected his own rich family. To Conrad, family relation is a class relation. He considers himself a family member or "a brother" of the poor, and he is dedicated to this big family and is ready to embrace the suffering brethren who do not have any biological relation with him. Mr. Dryfoos's remarks to his wife are resentful yet painfully earnest: "Well, I can tell him [Conrad] that charity begins at home. . . . And he'd better give himself to *us* a little—to his old father and mother. And his sisters" (232). Mr. Dryfoos desperately needs sympathy and love. He has a lot of money, but he feels that he is being "tied hand and foot." He is bewildered as he does not know which way to move (234). Margaret's sympathy toward the socially as well as financially destitute and her willingness to approach them help to eliminate barriers and create brotherly feelings among all social classes. She makes up for what is left not yet accomplished by Conrad, as exemplified in her visit to the Dryfoos family. Further, she provides Conrad with moral support and spiritual encouragement at the strike scene. Her love even dissolves Conrad's hatred and brings about his sympathy toward his father (420-21).

Among all the characters in the novel, March shows the greatest change from being a detached observer to a conscientious participant, from a transcendental esthete to a moral economist.[63] At the beginning of the novel, March, tolerant, generous, and well-cultivated in literature, is said to be "very sympathetic":

> . . . there was no good cause that they [Mr. and Mrs. March] did not wish well; they had a generous scorn of all kinds of narrow-heartedness; if it had ever come into their way to sacrifice themselves for others, they thought they would have done so, but they never asked why it had not come in their way. They were very gentle and kind, even when most elu-

> sive; and they taught their children to loathe all manner of social cruelty. (27)

However, March's sympathy for others is limited. When he and his wife catch sight of a decent-looking poor man on a New York street, March shows his mercy by giving a coin. But a trivial alm is the optimum help he can offer because he immediately withdraws from the grateful stranger (70-71). He would not unreservedly reach out, like Conrad and Margaret, to bridge the gap between the rich and the poor. When stricken with the miserable scenes in New York, March would go to the theater in order to "forget them" or make sketches to satisfy his esthetic needs (71, 147). Esthetic presentation of "those phases of low life" functions as a filter of painful misery and cruel reality. Even though March defends his own position by claiming that an ethical intention in literary creation would spoil his works, his apathetic stance is contrasted and underscored by Conrad's viewpoint.

> "If you can make the comfortable people understand how the uncomfortable people live, it will be a very good thing, Mr. March. Sometimes it seems to me that the only trouble is that we don't know one another well enough; and that the first thing is to do this." (147)

The novel carefully unfolds the change in the degree of March's sympathy by showing his gradually evolved views of poverty, money, and his role in the economic production. In New York, he strolls along the streets and observes people of heterogeneous backgrounds. He takes the car with Neapolitans who "worked and fed and housed like beasts" (182); he sees poor Chinese dwellers walking along the dirty pavement (185); and he encounters people of "shabby adversity" of "foreign birth" (183). As he gets to be more and more acquainted with these people, the social gap begins to reduce, and his perception shows an increasing understanding and compassion in him. The different complexion and features of the New Yorkers in sight give him suggestions for "the more public-spirited reveries in which he dealt with the future economy of our heterogeneous commonwealth" (183). His gazing at these scenes initiates his concern with the poor and their future:

> It must be owned that he did not take much trouble about this; what these poor people were thinking, hoping, fearing, enjoying, suffering; just where and how they lived; who and what they individually were—

> These were the matters of his waking dreams as he stared hard at them, while the train raced further into the gay ugliness—the shapeless, graceless, reckless picturesqueness of the Bowery. (183)

Some words are strangely juxtaposed in the last part: "gay" vs. "ugliness," "picturesqueness" vs. its three modifiers, that is, "the shapeless, graceless, reckless." These juxtapositions indicate the very changes in March. He still perceives the apparently unpleasant poverty-stricken scene, yet he has developed some new esthetic taste which enables him to recognize the picturesqueness in such a view. The "ugliness" is no longer threatening; instead, it appears interesting and friendly to someone who is observing sympathetically. In short, these words suggest a new perception with a balance of the moral and esthetics in consequence of the growth of sympathy.

Likewise, March's view of capital undergoes change. He used to be a defender of millionaires. Manifesting a rather sympathetic attitude toward millionaires, he tended to believe that some of these *nouveaux riches* made their fortunes in an honest way, and he would praise them for giving works to "armies of poor people" (191). As he gets to know Dryfoos better, his admiration of the millionaire gives way to a sour denunciation. March begins to recognize that Dryfoos has "undergone a moral deterioration" with his quick fortunes accumulated. He observes that Dryfoos has forfeited many valuable and respected qualities, such as intellectual ability, wisdom, and courage. He says, ". . . I am not very proud when I realize that such a man and his experience are the ideal and ambition of most Americans. I rather think they came pretty near being mine, once" (224-25). More significant is that March now recognizes his role in the literary corporation of *Every Other Week*. He now understands that the capitalist "that holds the purse holds the reins" (225). The editors are merely instrumental in producing profits for Dryfoos. They serve Dryfoos just like driving a wagon for him, and they can be replaced at any moment.

It needs to be emphasized, however, that March, though being more detached from the rich, can never resolutely dissolve his social and economic connection with the rich. March confesses, "We all respect money," and he supposes that philanthropic deeds are all supported by some "vile little motive" (278). For this reason, he considers Dryfoos's money in publishing the magazine as "an honorable use" (286), and regards the Dryfooses as "the raw material of good society" (278). Even so, March's stance is different from the other characters' in the novel mainly because March has obtained an understanding of both the rich and the poor. And he perceives the "intermingling of the fates of the mass."[64]

The ending of the novel demonstrates Howells's judicious and economical arrangement, with Conrad's death as a catalyst leading toward the completion of the structure and thematic development, a movement toward evoking sympathy for the destitute.[65] The significance of Conrad's death is only lightly suggested through March's questioning, "Perhaps he [Conrad] was of use in dying. Who knows?" (431). Yet Conrad's death has a decisive weight with March in his forming a more balanced view between esthetics and morality, and the ending follows the line of the thesis: give voice to the suppressed, find a channel of communication between the rich and poor, and change the economy that depreciates brotherly feelings. To this extent, the novel has drawn a remarkable and satisfactory conclusion.

March demonstrates a clear shift in the ending toward a humanitarian concern with the mass. He gives up his art-for-art stance, manifests his moral decisions, gets involved in the strike on the street, and becomes a participant in economic and ideological conflicts. At the beginning of the railroad strike, March shows a deep concern with the public interests. But his view indicates that he is really politically detached. March displays his discontent with both the property owners and the strikers.

> "The roads and the strikers are allowed to fight out a private war in our midst—as thoroughly and precisely a private war as any we despise the Middle Ages for having tolerated—as any street war in Florence or Verona—and to fight it out at our pains and expense, and we stand by like sheep, and wait till they get tired." (407)

March complains that both "the roads" and "the strikers" have got rights to fight their "private war" while "the public has no rights" to enjoy peace and safety. His attitude toward the strikers, however, differs significantly from Fulkerson's and Beaton's. Unlike Dryfoos, Woodburn, Fulkerson and Beaton, March has never suggested that the workers should be arrested, "put down with an iron hand," or executed against a wall in order to protect property rights and social order, though he complains that the strikers have caused turmoil in the city (404, 406, 408). He is concerned with the two million inhabitants of New York City and their "funny attitude" of being absurdly passive in their reaction to the turmoil.

It is this dissatisfaction with "the apparent indifference of the mighty city" that draws March to the strike scene. And it is his presence at the strike scene that eventually changes his view of the strikers. On the Second Avenue, March watches the strikers at "a safe distance" while a car laden with policemen comes down the track, but none of the strikers attacks it.

> In their simple Sunday best, March thought them very quiet, decent-looking people, and he could well believe that they had nothing to do with the riotous outbreaks in other parts of the city. He could hardly believe that there were any such outbreaks; he began more and more to think them mere newspaper exaggerations in the absence of any disturbance, or the disposition to it, that he could see. (411)

His witnessing of the strike dramatically shortens his distance with the workers who fight for minimum wages and sustenance. They appear to be "decent-looking" people, neither violent nor riotous. Contrasted with the policemen in the car, these workers seem extraordinarily humane and worthy of sympathy.

It is the sight of Conrad's death and Lindau's wound at the strike scene that shocks March and brings about a final change in his attitude. March witnesses Lindau drop under the club of a policeman and sees the dead body of Conrad beside the old man. Prior to the strike, March decided to keep himself away from Lindau, whose political and economic ideas had enraged Dryfoos. However, March is now both factually and symbolically left alone with Lindau and Conrad at the scene. Their misfortune brings him to deep grief, and his voice of sympathy is heard in his defence of Lindau, "He's a man of the most generous instincts, and a high ideal of justice, of equity—too high to be considered by a policeman with a club in his hand" (430). March realizes that "it would be useless to protest that his share of the calamity was, by comparison, infinitesimally small" (430). In other words, March is no longer an apathetic detached observer. Lindau's fatal wound and Conrad's death have linked March's fate with the labor movement and society.

Conrad's death has also triggered a ferocious demand for law, justice, and social order. March's confrontation with Dryfoos and Fulkerson before the strike has dispelled the complacent delusion that he is working for the manager Fulkerson and is not owned by the tyrannous Dryfoos. Now he understands that the will of Dryfoos, who owns the magazine, is the law. The magazine, though supposed to create mutual understandings, does not tolerate any sympathy toward Lindau or the poor; while it is supposed to act like an insurance company, letting everyone share an equal opportunity, it coerces the editors and contributors for meek consent. After Conrad's death, March, for the first time, openly and eloquently condemns, what he calls, the "economic chance world," in which one is subject to "the caprice, the mood, the indigestion" of the money power (436, 437).

> "It ought to be law as inflexible in human affairs as the order of day and night in the physical world, that if a man will work he shall both rest and eat, and shall not be harassed with any question as to how his repose and his provision shall come." (436)

Without such a law, there would be no security and justice. And March concludes his remarks by stating that

> ". . . when we get to the end, covered with blood and dirt and sin and shame, and look back over the way we've come to a palace of our own, or the poorhouse, which is about the only possession we can claim in common with our brother-men, I don't think the retrospect can be pleasing." (437)

March's uncertainty in his ending in "a palace" or "the poor house" further stresses the sense of insecurity, and it points toward the two extremes in social divisions in the future as well. March's view, supported by his wife, echoes Gronlund's and Bellamy's in their demand for an utopian society. March, who used to be enwrapped in a concern with his own microscopic world, has developed a critical and sympathetic vision which extends to the whole society and tries to transcend time and space to structure an ideal world in the future.

Conrad's death is transformed into a strong call for tolerance and embracing of heterogeneous voices. The editorial board of the magazine consists of those with sharply distinguished ideological views. But these views are tolerated as long as they are supportive of or unthreatening to the existing political apparatus or the economic interests of capital. When Lindau disrupts the symphonious conversation at the dinner table with his jarring opinion, cursing Dryfoos as "tyrant" and advocating a state of "the whole people" to replace the capitalist system (343, 344), he has transgressed the limit of tolerance and can no longer be allowed to serve as part of the magazine. Conrad's death brings about the reconciliation between both Conrad and Dryfoos, and Lindau and Dryfoos. Dryfoos comes to March and pleads with him to tell Lindau that he did not object to Lindau's ideas. He tells March that he has discovered Conrad's diary, which reveals that Conrad used to share Lindau's notions, equally incomprehensible to Dryfoos. This recalls the quarrel between Conrad and Dryfoos preceding Conrad's death, in which Dryfoos violently struck his son, who defended the right of the strikers: "I pity them; my whole heart is with those poor men" (418). At the time, Conrad was not allowed to voice his own opinion in front of his father, who believes that whoever owns has the say. Conrad's death and his diary evoke Dryfoos's sympathy toward both Conrad and Lindau. While acknowledging that he and Conrad differ in many aspects, Dryfoos repents that he "wasn't very good" toward the latter (448). He decides to carry on Conrad's humanitarianism and shows a willingness to embrace Lindau's heterogeneity as a gesture of recompense and reconciliation. All his hostility toward this radically critical socialist has now given way to a generosity or even gratefulness.

> "I don't feel any hardness to him because it was him that got Coonrod killed, as you might say, in one sense of the term; but I've tried to think it out, and I feel like I was all the more beholden to him because my son died tryin' to save him." (448-49)

Dryfoos offers to do whatever he can to help Lindau. Later he insists on having Lindau's funeral at his home, a symbolic gesture of accepting Lindau as part of his family.

The true value of Conrad's death can be better appreciated by placing it in relation to the theme of sympathy.[66] Conrad's death is unquestionably an unrecoverable loss. March ponders over the value of Conrad's death and says, "I used to think the world was appreciably richer for his being in it. But are we appreciably poorer for his being out of it now?" (442). Similarly, Fulkerson, lamenting Conrad's death, shows his appreciation of Conrad as "a precious creature."

> "And what a lot of the raw material of all kinds the Almighty must have, to *waste* us the way he seems to do. Think of throwing away a precious creature like Coonrod Dryfoos on one chance in a thousand of getting

> that old fool of a Lindau out of the way of being clubbed!" (442)

By selecting such terms as "the raw material of all kinds," "waste," "precious," and "getting," Fulkerson seems to be calculating and planning a wiser arrangement, that is, with a minimum cost for a maximum profit. He concludes definitively that Conrad has wasted his life in saving Lindau, the "old fool." Nevertheless, the world is not "appreciably poorer" and neither has Conrad wasted his life. Limited by his selfishness and disesteem for Lindau, Fulkerson fails to perceive the subsequent chain of "profit" germinated by Conrad's death.

Conrad's death paradoxically initiates a call for sympathy and the universal law of love. Dryfoos now regrets that he failed to allow Conrad to be a preacher. But he does not realize that Conrad, with his diary left behind and with his love shown in saving Lindau, has become a successful preacher. Conrad's voice is now heard and accepted by Dryfoos, the Marches, and other people around. And this communication is essential in creating an understanding and sympathy, or tolerating and welcoming heterogeneous viewpoints in society. March finally understands that Conrad did have "some business" at the strike scene: the "business to suffer there for the sins of others" (452). Conrad becomes a modern Christ figure, healing the sick and suffering for the sins of others. His self-sacrifice, which is based on love for mankind, is a form of unconditional giving and sharing. Conrad has set a model for the society to follow in order to establish religious orders and breed feelings of brotherhood. March comments,

> "If we love mankind, pity them, we even *wish* to suffer for them. That's what has created the religious orders in all times—the brotherhoods and sisterhoods that belong to our day—as much as to the mediaeval past." (452)

In a word, Conrad's death is converted to an emotional call for the law of love and for sympathy among all social classes, both rich and poor. Dryfoos generously transfers his ownership of the magazine to Fulkerson and March, and allows them to manage the magazine in whatever way they want. March and Fulkerson eventually have the freedom to run a business and do not need to fear the power of the tyrannous owner who knows nothing about literature and art.

Nevertheless, ambiguity and dissatisfaction are there in the very clarity and satisfaction of the conclusion. In this seemingly neat solution to the problems of selfishness in the chance world, some details seem arbitrarily arranged, and some key issues left in suspense. The future of the magazine, for example, may not be as optimistic as expected since Beaton has again been included and the fact that Fulkerson is addressed as "the ownah" points to some potential feud in the future. Lindau is being honored and sympathized with, but the fact that he is dead helps to keep his views safely alienated, in exactly the same way as Woodburn's view of the defunct slavery system, which can constitute no more threat. Even Conrad's timely death, with its value recognized, seems arbitrary and calculated in order to solve all the conflicts. These details—Lindau's timely death as a way to ensure harmony; Dryfoos's generous withdrawal to give capital and autonomy to Fulkerson and March; and Conrad's death to awaken sympathy as well as to lift March out of the dilemma regarding Lindau's position at the magazine (357)—are signs of a utopian treatment of the irresolvable social conflicts. And this utopian treatment exposes the very problem of Howells's realism, and it registers his ambivalence toward the capitalist economy.

It is worth recalling at this point Howells's famous essay "The Man of Letters as A Man of Business" published in 1902. In the essay, Howells discusses the role of the writer and the way to achieve success in a competitive literary market. Uncertainty, ambiguity, and ambivalence are the outstanding features of the essay. Howells complains that literature has only "subjective value." And this value is subject to the mood or taste of the reader, and it can never be "fairly marketed." Reader's acceptance thus becomes the only determinant of this value, and this value is unpredictable and "wholly uncertain" from month to month.[67] As a successful writer and a mentor, Howells advises young writers that they should keep out of mind the opinion of the reader and the public, and attempt to please only themselves. This will be "better taste" and "better business" because, if they do so, they will "very probably please other people."[68]

In its essence, Howells's advice to alleviate uncertainty in this haphazard business world is to be a sympathetic writer. The best writers are "men of aesthetic conscience and of generous sympathy."[69] Earlier in 1886, Howells also stated that the aim of the realistic novel is to "widen the bounds of sympathy" to proclaim the "equality of things and the unity of men."[70] Trying to forget the reader and keep a focused interest on one's own, according to Howells, may be adopted as a strategy to touch and please the heart of the reader and eventually win the reader through a sympathetic sharing. To put it another way, success lies in an understanding and pleasing of one's own feelings which will be extended to and shared by the public.

Howells is not just discussing his opinion of esthetic taste and literary value; he is unfolding his theory of realism. A three-party-relationship is formulated: the public, the writer, and the self. To touch and to please the public, a writer should first please himself. Notice that, in his demand, Howells implies that writing is not really a solitary activity. A writer is simultaneously one who writes to please and one who is to be pleased. And this act of pleasing is a social activity, since it aims to arouse pleasure and sympathy in the public eventually.

Howells's theory is reminiscent of Adam Smith's "impartial spectator" theory which describes the complex social relationship that observation and sympathy may generate. Likewise, this social relationship consists of three parties: the "spectator," the sympathy-provider, and the sympathy-receiver.

> Generosity, humanity, kindness, compassion, mutual friendship and esteem, all the social and benevolent affections, when expressed in the countenance or behaviour, even towards those who are not peculiarly connected with ourselves, please the indifferent spectator upon almost every occasion. His sympathy with the person who feels those passions, exactly coincides with his concern for the person who is the object of them. The interest, which, as a man, he is obliged to take in the happiness of this last, enlivens his fellow-feeling with the sentiments of the other, whose emotions are employed about the same subject.[71]

The "indifferent spectator" is induced by the sight to feel sympathetic with the other two parties, and mutual feelings reduce social barriers and bring people together. The relationship among these three parties involved coincides with the counterpart in Howells's theory.

The three-party-relationship, which is Howells's theory of realism, operates in *Hazard*. When Dryfoos reads Conrad's diary, he is playing the role of a spectator, metaphorically observing Conrad's giving sympathy to the suffering majority of the society. Similarly, at the strike scene, March witnesses Lindau being struck by the policeman and Conrad lying dead next to the old man. His observation of Lindau fighting for the benefit of the poor produces some unnameable force in March, "stronger than his will" and drawing him closer to the innocent victims. These observations effectively eliminate the social distance between the "spectator" and the objects and effect the changes at the end of the novel. Likewise, Howells, who continued to search for "law and justice," wrote the novel to show his sympathy toward the Haymarket martyrs. The novel was to circulate in the market, and it should arouse the sympathy of the public (who play the role of "indifferent spectator") for the anarchists and "the struggling mass."[72]

Howells's dependence upon sympathy, together with the traces of arbitrariness in the conclusion of the novel, are indicative of ambivalence and confusion, originating from Howells's own political theory and his economic life.[73] Even though he was a consistent critic of a money-oriented America, Howells cherished hope in reform. He sympathized with the innocent martyrs of the Haymarket tragedy and the workers during their strikes of the nineties, but he insisted on the vision of America being peacefully transformed into a benign socialist society, as echoed by Basil March in the novel. Why should the workers employ violence when they could resort to more peaceful means to have a fare share of the profits of industry? In short, he regarded sympathy as a progressive means to reform the socioeconomic system and better human relationships, for amelioration, not for a complete change. Besides, Howells's personal success in the chance economy was also a partial cause. Howells was "a remorselessly efficient literary machine—whose output was highly profitable."[74] He became one of the wealthiest writers after the publication of *The Rise of Silas Lapham* (1885). His net worth in 1890, the year when *Hazard* was published, rose to $60,000, a figure steadily growing in the 1890s, while many Americans were experiencing financial hardships.[75] He was certainly a man of letters as well as a man of business, and his success in both productivity and popularity was generally known and worthy of the envy of even a shrewd businessman. The confusion in his concern with the inequalities of American society was frankly acknowledged by the writer himself in his letter to his father, dated February 2, 1890.

> [Mark Twain] and his wife and Elinor and I are all of accord in our way of thinking: that is, we are theoretical socialists, and practical aristo-

> crats. But it is a comfort to be right theoretically, and to be ashamed of one's self practically.[76]

He could advocate socialist ideas, but he could never truly sever himself from the luxury and prestige he enjoyed as a successful writer. And prior to this, on October 10, 1888, Howells revealed a similar trace of ambivalence in his letter to Henry James:

> I should hardly like to trust pen and ink with all the audacity of my social ideas; but after fifty years of optimistic content with "civilization" and its ability to come out all right in the end, I now abhor it, and feel that it is coming out all wrong in the end, unless it bases itself anew on a real equality. Meantime, I wear a fur-lined overcoat, and live in all the luxury my money can buy.[77]

Hazard as a realistic novel clearly indicates Howells's direct responses to the Haymarket event and his attempt to create a tie of sympathy among all social classes. The ambivalence toward the social and economic system as shown in the ending and the form of the novel are most suggestive and meaningful. As both a cultural contender and a beneficiary, Howells, when making criticism of self-interest, can never be whole-hearted.

Chapter III

Economy of Attention: *The Cliff-Dwellers* and *With the Procession*

In Henry Blake Fuller's *With the Procession* (1895), Mrs. Susan Bates assists Mrs. Eliza Marshall in arranging her daughter Rosy Marshall's coming-out party. On the following day, Mrs. Bates instructs Jane Marshall, the elder daughter of the family, to make no rearrangement in their rooms because things there are "in perfect agreement." Mrs. Bates assures Jane that they have "a low, quiet tone," which is "the best" and "the hardest thing to get."[1] Mrs. Bates further instructs them to put a slice of lemon in every cup to prevent the guests from drinking much tea and being distracted. Mrs. Bates's idea seems to Jane more than absurd, and the latter bursts into laughter.

> "But ma doesn't want to discourage her friends."
> "My good girl," said Mrs. Bates, impressively, "this whole function has only one object. That object is to show your sister for five minutes to Cecilia Ingles."
> "Oh, that's it?"
> "That's it, and all of it." (106)

If the function of the party is truly to show Rosy "for five minutes to Cecilia Ingles," the Marshalls and Mrs. Bates surely succeed in accomplishing this task later. Though the information regarding Rosy's performance is as brief as Cecilia Ingles's stay, Fuller tactfully sheds light on Ingles's viewpoint of the party. After showing that beautiful Rosy flashes and glitters in the "dim and depressing old parlor" like "a garnet set in dull gold," Fuller writes,

> Cecilia Ingles, who could not but admire her beauty and readiness, thought that her tone was a little too hard, and that in her excess of aplomb she pushed self-possession to the verge of self-assertion. (106)

The lines that Fuller places immediately following this seem both natural and confounding:

> Rosy, in fact, entered society not with the tentative step and slow advance of one who cautiously feels an unaccustomed way, but by a single confident and intuitive leap. (106)

It seems natural since Fuller appears to be introducing the consequence of a successful debut party. However, it simultaneously strikes one as confounding because of the sequential connection of these facts: Ingles's attendance, her comment, and Rosy's instant success. Fuller sets them in such a way that Rosy's success—entering society by "a single confident and intuitive leap"—is shown to be the consequence of Ingles's attendance at the party. To put it another way, Ingles's attention is the magical abracadabra that has brought instant success to Rosy.

Attention means "earnest direction of the mind, consideration, or regard."[2] Ingles's attention, however, is presented as something as valuable as, or more valuable than, money. Later in the novel, Susan Bates tells Arthur Paston about a conversation she had with Ingles prior to the Bateses' house party. Attention and money are compared and evaluated by Mrs. Bates:

> "The first thing she asked me was how much money I wanted. 'I dont [sic] want any of your money at all,' I told her; 'for such a cause as this I can scoop up all the money I want by the shovelful. No; what I want is your personal interest.' That's about the hardest thing to get in cases like this." (229)

Attention circulates in the giving-and-getting form like specie. The attention from Ingles can be more important and decisive than money to Susan Bates, a millionaire's wife.

How to get more attention from Ingles and the public is really what Rosy Marshall or Susan Bates are concerned with. It is, actually, what *The Cliff-Dwellers* (1893) and *With the Procession*—Fuller's two reputable Chicago novels—are concerned with. Fuller, in his presentation of nineteenth-century Chicago, successfully depicts the economy of attention—the predominant phenomenon of attention-seeking—and thus presents a realistic picture of the era near the turn of the century.[3]

Thorstein Veblen, Fuller's contemporary and an unusually cynical social theorist at the University of Chicago, gives a biting and satirical criticism of the *nouveau riche* in his renowned work *The Theory of the Leisure Class* (1899). Veblen points out that people in modern society habitually make distinctions between industrial and non-industrial occupations, or working and leisure classes, and this "modern distinction is a transmuted form of the barbarian distinction between exploit and drudgery."[4] To Veblen, modern society is still a predatory phase of culture, although it has witnessed a gradual evolution and cumulative growth of "predatory attitudes, habits, and traditions."[5] The leisure class endeavors to distinguish itself from the laboring class by excelling in pecuniary standing and in a variety of economic expressions. Veblen writes, "The basis on which good repute in any highly organized industrial community ultimately rests is pecuniary strength; and the means of showing pecuniary strength, and so of gaining or retaining a good name, are leisure and a conspicuous consumption of goods."[6]

Even though Veblen never uses the term "attention-seeking" in his criticism of the hollowness of the canons of taste, dress, or education of the leisure class, what he means to anatomize, expose, and stigmatize is this very phenomenon. He has coined and applied such terms as "pecuniary emulation," "conspicuous leisure," "conspicuous consumption," or "invidious distinction,"[7] each of which economically recapitulates one aspect of the phenomenon. Actually early in 1894, when Fuller was writing his second Chicago novel, Veblen already launched his critique in "The Economic Theory of Woman's Dress," a revised version of which was later included in *The Theory of the Leisure Class*. Dress, as Veblen argues, originally had the principal function of adornment, and over the years it has gradually evolved and become "the index of the wealth" represented by the wearer. The three principles of women's dress are "expensiveness," "novelty," and "ineptitude." Dress, in other words, offers "*prima facie* evidence" of the wearer's economic group's capability of purchasing expensive and luxurious items, "inability to withstand any appreciable amount of wear," and freedom from any practical, productive occupation. Even the esthetic value of the dress becomes subservient, like a "handmaid," to the "principle of novelty."[8]

In the 1890s, millionaires in Chicago, Boston, New York, and other major cities were admired and envied for the enormous amount of their personal possessions. Quantity had become the measurement for greatness, and money the sign of success, the symbol of status, and the source of a cult. The rich lavishly spent their money on the large and concrete; they even imported masterpieces and even whole castles from European countries. The obvious and massive were thus promoted to meet the quest for goodness in bigness. The Vanderbilts, in the midst of an economic depression, built their summer homes, one of which was a $5 million palace of seventy rooms with thirty-three house servants, and the other a $2 million villa plus furnishings which were worth $9 million.[9] Mrs. Potter Palmer, who was well aware of the necessity to create a distinctive public image, built the "most imposing house" in Chicago where she entertained visiting royalty during the Columbian Exposition. Visitors would pass "a French drawing room, a Spanish music room, an English dining room . . . or through a Moorish corridor into a Turkish parlor or perhaps a Greek or Japanese parlor" before they saw Mrs. Palmer's "Louis XVI bed ten feet high." The glow of her Impressionist painting collection in her gallery could outshine any other private collectors in the world.[10]

Chicago, in which Fuller's two novels unfold, enjoyed an extravagant period of economic and cultural growth from 1880 to 1892. It became, in Fuller's words, "a 'producing centre' of—extravaganza."[11] The eminent industrialists and merchants there caught the attention of the nation. The packinghouses boomed and steel production quickly soared, second to Pittsburgh only. Some impressive cultural institutions—the Art Institute, the Auditorium Theater, and the University of Chicago—were established. Together with these developments came the rapid construction of skyscrapers. After the Great Chicago Fire of 1871, many outstanding architects, attracted by the opportunity to rebuild Chicago, came and displayed their ingenuity in endowing the city with a breathtaking new feature. *Morris' Dictionary of Chicago* defined the Chicago in 1891 as "a city of 'skyscrapers.'" No other city in the nation could claim "the general high average of elegant and massive buildings" as Chicago.[12]

Surely skyscrapers attracted the attention of the public. Grand entrances, embellished lobbies, rich marbles, mosaics, hardwoods, and ornamental ironworks were common features of the skyscrapers, and these features distinguished the buildings from other earlier and plainer structures in the city. With their expensive materials and the glimmer of new styles, these high-rises were no longer merely for sheltering the inhabitants; they began to serve as a mark, an indicator of wealth and social stratification. These buildings, with their grand entrances, decorations, and seemingly nondiscriminatory hospitality, welcomed all visitors to take their elevators and move about. Many businesses were happy to be associated with such a massive, eye-catching structure.

The skyscraper, with its accentuating beauty and size, appeared to be promoting democracy. It was a miniature of social and commercial world, where everyone seemed to be welcomed. Yet the rise of the skyscraper made attention-seeking a necessity and showed that social equality was merely a utopian social construct. Inside the skyscraper's iron and steel structure, built with standardized components, human beings were interlocked in complex relationships and many fell into anonymity. It became critically important for everyone to be distinct and distinctive in order to climb the social ladder and be a success. The skyscraper, which often occupied a central position in the city, changed the landscape and marginalized those social failures. In Chicago, for example, the skyscraper became the "vortex" of the city.[13] Surrounded by the old city with its six- and eight-story buildings, the skyscraper attracted thousands of people into the heart of the city every day. In the meantime, however, slums and tenement houses sprawled around. Jane Addams and other social reformers created Hull House and other settlement houses to provide sympathy and fight poverty, and to help new immigrants. The contrast between the skyscraper and its surrounding areas must have been astounding, though the skyscraper covered the adjacent slum areas with its giant shadow.

The World's Columbian Exposition in 1893, Chicago's triumph in national competition to celebrate the four-hundredth anniversary of the discovery of America, marked the climax in the material and architectural extravagance. The World's Fair attracted the nation's leading architects, who designed the colossal and magnificent palaces in the Court of Honor, with a great fountain in the center. These buildings, together with the surrounding halls, displayed the industrial potential power. In these buildings, international achievements in mining, agriculture, machinery, and electricity were exhibited. The design of the Court of Honor was in a neoclassical style. Nearly all the buildings were of colossal size, and some of them were the largest structures ever built. The Manufactures and Liberal Arts Building, with its forty-four acres of floor space, was said to be large enough to contain the United States Capitol, the Great Pyramid, Winchester Cathedral, Madison Square Garden, and St. Paul's Cathedral. Uniform cornice height, glaring snowy white color, and monumental features of these buildings brought them the popular name "White City."[14] On May 1, 1893, as President Grover Cleveland pressed a golden, telegraph key, "ten thousand electric lights flashed on, the sprays of a dozen fountains shot into the air, a hundred flags unfurled, Thomas' Orchestra struck up the Columbian March. . . ." It was a sensation and a miracle, to the world as well as the million who assembled at the opening ceremony.[15]

The enchanting architecture of the World's Fair rightly earned Chicago the name of the "Dream City." Robert Herrick, a Chicago writer, said that the Fair was "Chicago, its dream, its ideal, its noblest self incarnated in magnificent building, in splendor of size and pomp and beauty."[16] The Fair infused in the public a wonderful, optimistic confidence: America, though sharply divided in wealth and stricken with constant economic turmoils and labor movements, could accomplish anything with its "love of the ideal of beauty."[17] Only a few years before, there was merely a wilderness of wet grass and mud flats. All of a sudden, numerous spectacular buildings were miraculously erected there on the lake. The harmonious cluster of these buildings, so different from the dirty city outside Jackson Park, seemed to have successfully eased all social tensions and merrily welcomed the large crowd of diversified visitors to the World's Fair. Theodore Dreiser marvelled at the architecture of the Fair. He believed that the splendid picturesque Fair, like a "dream of beauty," must have opened even the pessimists' eyes. He went so far that he even called the Fair a "fairyland" that the "magic wand" of some brooding spirit of beauty had brought about.[18] To Dreiser, the Fair seemed to be "a symbol of what the city was not rather than what it was."[19]

But it was precisely the Fair's being "what the city was not" that made the Fair a symbol of the city and the nation. The Renaissance and neoclassical style that brought the grandiosity to the Fair was nothing but a by-product of the dominant social motif of attention-seeking. The architects of the Beaux-Arts Society, who rejected and mocked Louis Sullivan's theory of architecture, constructed most of the buildings in an imitation of ancient formalism. The exterior impressed the visitors with its "ordered monumentality," a feature that became characteristic of the public space, such as the museum, the gallery, and the department store.[20] Yet the exterior of these buildings—decorous and majestic—was contrasted with the interior, which housed the exhibitions that suggested profusion and variety. Frank Lloyd Wright criticized the architecture design of the Fair as the sign of the "nervous artificiality of the 'classic' grandiomania." The Fair, to him as well as to Sullivan, was a tragedy. Wright said that "the florid countenance" of the Beaux-Arts and perversion of their practice brought "a blight" upon the progress of the nation.[21] Sullivan's pointed remarks were even more penetrating: The World's Fair was simply a deadly "virus" and an "appalling calamity," and its damage would "last for half a century from its date, if not longer."[22]

Fuller demonstrates his strong interest in the World's Fair in his numerous sketches between 1892 and 1893.[23] Overall he is optimistic and passionate in his presentation of the magnificent architecture of the World's Fair. He affirms the progress in the area of architecture, which has displayed "considerable invention and ingenuity" and advanced "at an equal pace" with the industry. He is very proud of the plan developed by Daniel Hudson Burnham and John W. Root, which helped to lay the "ground" for the success of the Fair. He enthusiastically values the systematic organization, collective efforts, and common understanding among the architects, which should be a model to follow for future architects of other buildings.[24]

In the same article, Fuller compares the Fair with the Paris exhibition in 1889, a comparison that highlighted the feature of conspicuousness and grandiosity. Chicago, as Fuller notes, "will compare herself with only the latest, the biggest, the best." Its Fair has "much more numerous," "larger," and "more splendid" buildings than the Paris exhibition.[25] Fuller then comments:

> But there is one consideration that should curb our pride. These Paris buildings were real buildings—are, for they still stand and serve various purposes. Our buildings are not real buildings; they are only models of buildings—simulacra of buildings. They stand out like a beautiful dream, but the dream will come to an end soon, as all dreams do and must.[26]

The passage ironically undercuts the author's sincerity in identifying the splendor of the Fair. By naming the faddism, emulation, and evanescence as well as the pomposity of the architecture, Fuller suddenly shifts his stance toward that of a bitter observer, pointing out the feature of "attention-seeking" of the Fair.

A few years later, in "The Upward Movements in Chicago," the similar sanguine tone of the article is contrasted with the elements of sarcasm, suspicion, disappointment, and disapproval. The article gives a comprehensive picture of the city and an apparently favorable assessment of the progress of the city. Right in the beginning, Fuller writes,

> The opportunity to attempt a marshaling and review of some of the elements prominent in the composition of a large, new, and conspicuous community is not one to be accepted in a spirit of easy self-confidence; and when these elements are at once comprehensive in range, discordant in character, and so overcharged with peculiarities as to be rendered susceptible to a rather wide variety of interpretation, then the commentator can only approach them in a certain spirit of self-distrust.[27]

If the social reality is "discordant," Fuller certainly has demonstrated his ingenious mastery of literary skills in successfully recapitulating the "discordant" reality in this article. While showing with patriotic pride the construction of cultural institutions in Chicago to the world, Fuller abhors skyscrapers, which, to him, abuse "private initiative" and have no artistic value; while cheering the cultural development that has given birth to a "Literary Chicago," Fuller slashes the vulgarity of the city, where "scale"—such as the extensive scale of the Fair—has become the sole measurement of success; while praising Chicago's ability to draw the attention of the world, Fuller remarks that the city has been devoted, "through too many years, to ideals essentially false."[28] In Chicago's architecture in particular Fuller recognizes "the picturesque flagrancy" that also characterizes the city. In the end, Fuller's tone changes to affirmative and sanguine. Fuller specifies "the extirpation of the moral and civic evil" as the principal concern of the next generation in this city which has gained its "final supremacy, commercial, intellectual, and political."[29]

The phenomenon of attention-seeking was really a general cultural motif, not limited to the circle of the leisure class only. The American culture in the nineteenth century, with industrial development and expansion, transformed itself from the eighteenth century "Self-Culture"—one that emphasized self-improvement as represented in the case of Benjamin

Franklin—to "Self-Promotion" through "Winning Images."[30] At the turn of the century, when corporations and modern industry gained a rigid control of the society in every aspect, the bureaucratization of the corporate career swerved the path of self-advancement for ambitious young men. As the cultural historian Christopher Lasch points out, these young venturers had to compete with their peers for "the attention and approval of their superiors." In their rivalry and struggle against their peer competitors, they no longer sought, or adhered to, conventional Puritan work ethics; rather they depended on "will-power, self-confidence, energy, and initiative." And they were imitating the successful, and creating and adjusting their own images in the eyes of the public. They knew that success was "ratified by publicity,"[31] and personal appearance and public image played a decisive role in success. Personal obscurity meant vanishing and failure, and keeping oneself constantly in view would lead to success.

The emphasis on attention and the determination to win success through gaining attention were vigorously promoted by cultural organs. By the end of the nineteenth century, self-help books, for example, became popular as they boosted will-power and successfully catered to the needs of the consumer. They were "dominated by the ethos of salesmanship and boosterism."[32] In their advice to the young followers, these self-help popularizers shared an agreement in defining the prerequisite for success: personal magnetism. As a quality that enabled a man to influence others, personal magnetism became "one of the major keys to success."[33] In George Horace Lorimer's popular book, *Letters from a Self-Made Merchant to His Son* (1903), John Graham, a pork baron, gives advice to his son Pierrepont, who studies at Harvard and then becomes a successful businessman. To Graham, the traditional religion, ethics, and morals are appealing only when they are useful in reaching the goal of personal success and distinction. He conceives of education as a useful tool in reaching the goal because it makes one quick to think and to outwit competitors, and he stresses energy and a strong will. Most striking of all is the fact that Graham underlines the need to build a "dynamic personality" to attract attention in a large organization. To win others' attention, in short, is imperative in gaining success.[34]

Another example is John Walker Harrington's "Ottenhausen's Coup," a story published in *McClure's Magazine* in 1898. Carl Ottenhausen, a young chemist, has just arrived to work as an analyzer at Laird's Furnace of the Mingo Coal and Iron Company. On the second night, while he is taking charge of the iron furnace, some anarchists organize a revolt. Ottenhausen, awe-inspiring, with two revolvers in his hands, confronts the thirty rebellious workers and suppresses the revolt. The supervisor and the manager of the company, who happen to be at a party nearby, quickly arrive at the scene. Ottenhausen is assured later by the supervisor that he will not always be a chemist because the manager has witnessed "the whole business." As predicted, Ottenhausen is elevated soon afterwards from the valley where the iron furnace is located to the top of a skyscraper. The story thus concludes,

> In the top of a tall building in Columbus there is a door bearing a porcelain label which reads: "General Manager." Behind that door sits Carl Ottenhausen, who now directs the destinies of the Mingo Coal and Iron Company.[35]

Attention, which has brought Rosy to instant success, is reaffirmed as a critical determinant in Ottenhausen's case.

Andrew Carnegie, one of the most renowned tycoons in the nineteenth century, also defends the phenomenon of "attention-seeking" in his article "Wealth," which was published in 1889.[36] Carnegie explicates and praises the law of competition, which he acclaims as beneficial to the whole race and to the future progress of society. He states that American society provides great scope for "the exercise of special ability" in the merchants and manufacturers, and it generously rewards those who possess and apply the rare talent for organization and management. By the same token, those who are incapable of earning even interest upon their capital deserve to be bankrupt. In his discussion of individualism, Carnegie upholds individual distinction as measured by one's economic achievement. Carnegie reveres the wealthy as a precious species. He argues that the most talented and diligent in achieving financial success deserve to be respected and distinguished while the weak should fall into anonymity.[37]

Andrew Carnegie, in his interview with Theodore Dreiser in 1899, specifically underlines attention-seeking as an effective strategy for young men to rise in society. He rejects the widely accepted belief that the society does not offer many opportunities to the ambitious beginners and success has become impossible. He states that a rising man should not just accomplish the assigned duties; he should do "something exceptional, and beyond the range of his special department." Carnegie then explains that a shippage clerk, for example, may discover in an invoice an error which has escaped the attention of the proper party, and the discovery may well bring the attention of the supervisor and consequently bring himself success. Carnegie does not mention at all those qualities merited by the eighteenth century "self-culture." To him, every service can be a vehicle for young men to display their usefulness, worthiness of trust, and invincible determination to rise.[38] The terse advice that the successful Carnegie gives is that one "must attract attention."[39]

Nevertheless, attention-seeking was also challenged and criticized by some cultural critics. Big cities, like Chicago, offered wonderful opportunities for anyone to rise and be a celebrity; but they also cultivated anonymity and obliterated individual identity. The story of the "charity girl" recorded in *The Gold Coast and the Slum* offers not hope but disappointment, and it questions the promise that the society seems to have made. The protagonist is a music prodigy from a small town in Kansas. After college, she does not want to go back to marry a "Babbitt" and live on "Main Street." Instead, she chooses to go to Chicago to pursue her study in music. But her aspiration soon evaporates as she gets entangled in various problems, among which the most unbearable is loneliness. She finds herself unable to make even a single friend in this huge city, and she feels the city lacks personal touch.

> In all this city of three million souls I knew no one, cared for no one, was cared for by no one. In a popular science story in the evening newspaper a few days before I had read how the universe is composed of millions of stars whirling about. I looked up at the sky. I was just like that—an atom whirled about with three million other atoms, day after day, month after month, year after year.[40]

Elements such as "loneliness," "desperation," and "triviality" find their resonance in quite a number of literary works by social critics who challenge the possibility of winning attention for gaining a foothold in social climbing. *Sister Carrie*, an encyclopedia of the Chicago at the turn of the century, bears such an astounding resemblance to the above mentioned story. Both Carrie and that anonymous "charity girl" come from a small town, suffer from loneliness, and are seduced by a married man. While the "charity girl" is deceived and then deserted, Carrie successfully moves on to the center of the stage and gains the public attention. But Dreiser's subtle irony and pessimistic tone can hardly be missed near the end of the story where Carrie is placed in her rocking chair by the window. Darkness and obscurity await like a dangerous monster to engulf Carrie once her youthful glamour loses its attraction and she the attention.

This socioeconomic phenomenon of attention-seeking in the late nineteenth century prompted sharp responses and attracted much attention of Chicago writers, among whom was Henry Blake Fuller. The symbolic function of the Clifton building and the stream of the procession in *The Cliff-Dwellers* and *With the Procession* have been emphasized by most critics. John Pilkington, Jr., for example, comments that the Clifton in *The Cliff-Dwellers* has provided Fuller "with both an enveloping form and a controlling idea to which everything else in the novel might have been related."[41] And Bernard R. Bowron, Jr., shows what Fuller has called "architectural order" in the novel: most of the chapters are of the same length, like a solid edifice, devoid of verbosity.[42] In his comment on *With the Procession*, Robert C. Bray points out that the actual procession of traffic in downtown Chicago is analogous to the social and economic procession.[43] And Bray believes that the procession has "a fluidity and a freedom beyond . . . the socialized art of a towering building." It is a process "too vast and diffuse to be directed by the wills of Cecilia and Arthur Ingles."[44]

Truly, the skyscraper and the procession are dominating symbols in Fuller's Chicago novels. But the real significance of these two different symbols lies in their successful representation of the socioeconomic phenomenon of attention-seeking in Fuller's contemporary America. The two symbols allow Fuller to draw a panoramic picture of the interlocked social groups which rely upon and compete against each other for recognition and success.

Surely, the two symbols, because of their differences in nature, seem to operate in opposite directions. On the one hand, the Clifton, an eighteen-floor skyscraper, provides a vertical, uprising image. As the social and business center, it is solid and stable. The building both consolidates and confines its "cliff-dwellers." On the other hand, the procession brings up an image of a horizontal, forward movement. It suggests momentum, restlessness, progress, or "expansive possibilities for personal and national fulfillment."[45]

However, these two novels, despite the difference in their dominating symbols, share some important features. First, each of them shows a collective image of society in which individuals are moving either up or along. The struggle to move upward or forward, rather than standing still or falling behind, is stressed in both of these novels. Second, material display is a salient feature shared by both. The Clifton building in *The Cliff-Dwellers* strikes the world with its hundreds of windows, which "glitter with multitudinous lettering in gold and in silver, and on summer afternoons its awnings flutter score on score in the tepid breezes."[46] *With the Procession*, on the other hand, stresses explicitly the necessity of material display. Those who make "no pretence to fashion" will be left "a little behind," that is, being out of fashion and attention, and eventually out of the procession (*WP* 5). Third, both of these novels challenge the notion of progress. With the title *The Cliff-Dwellers*, Fuller suggests that living in skyscrapers, which have been hailed as a sign of civilization, is nothing but a continuation of the barbarous culture. Skyscrapers merely provide a roof to a "large and rather heterogeneous" "tribe" of four thousand souls to have their "tribal feast" or communicate with their "chiefs" (*CD* 4-5). Similarly, *With the Procession* raises this question: are we truly moving forward? The Marshalls are "far, very far indeed, from any attempt to cut a great figure," and they are thus confronted with the danger of dropping out of the progression. Fuller begins the novel with Marshall's deathbed scene, which sets a deplorable mourning tone. And this mood is reinforced by the large letter "M" distinctively displayed in the Marshall's carriage in the following scene near the bridge. Given the actual circumstance and the homophone "Marshal," the letter "M" may stand for "moving," "march," or just "maneuver"; yet the imminent death and the deplorable tone make "memory" and "mourning" equally possible implications (*WP* 5).

The two novels, with the same historical and geographical setting and a number of similar characters, are really similar despite the difference in their dominating symbols. Through these two novels, the social phenomenon of attention-seeking is masterfully presented. To Fuller, a book, like an architecture, is an integral construction, consisting of hundreds and thousands of components. Each of these components is equipollent and indispensable in its contribution to the formation of the overall structure. For this very reason, Fuller believes that a quick look at a few randomly selected pages of a book would be an efficient way to "form an opinion" of the book.[47] Every page of his two novels does bestow some fascinating new detail, offering a glimpse of this social phenomenon. Examples which depict material display and manners, two common aspects of attention-seeking, can be easily noted.

In the aspect of material exhibition of economic possessions, the most conspicuous are probably architecture and room decoration. The Clifton, built by Arthur Ingles, is a skyward "exhibit" of his wealth. And this enormous "exhibit" is composed of hundreds of small exhibit units, among which is the Massachusetts Brass Company on the tenth floor. Fuller thus describes the office of the company: "Indeed, there is cause enough for envy in that small square of velvety Axminster, in the harmonious tinting of the walls, in the padded leather backs of the swivel chairs, in the polished brightness of the cherry desk-tops, in the fresh blotting-pads and the immaculate inkstands" (*CD* 6). The pleasant business office also serves as an apartment, which offers "a perch" to visitors, often from families of social pillars in Boston or large land-owners in Wyoming and Dakota. They are always welcomed there to relax and enjoy the "possible luxury of business." These friends, neat in dress and calculated in conversation, would comment on their host. The place, as Fuller introduces, is "less a hive of industry than a social exchange" of wealth and material superiority (*CD* 7).

Displaying material possession is shown to be essential to business success. "In Chicago, business depends on its external show or impression." D. Walworth Floyd, the president of Massachusetts Brass Company, explains that People "go by what they see" (*CD* 234). The standard of sufficiency is hardly considered. Or rather, being sufficient means that the wealth and luxury of the owner is efficiently displayed. In Floyd's office, there are electrical devices on the wall for calling boys from everywhere, yet these devices are rarely implemented. They are used to create the impression of their being implemented and thus to help business. Creating impression rather than being practically useful has become the genuine function of these expensive devices.

Mrs. Susan Bates's house is another breath-taking "exhibit" of wealth: a spacious music room, which its hostess calls a "great barn of a place"; the sets of classics on the music-stand have been long undisturbed, and the grand piano has not been touched by the owner, who may not be able to play even a single note; in her library, a range of ornate bookcases with "utmost taste" and artistic skill are loaded with formal and costly bindings: Dickens, Thackeray, Bulwer, Hume, Gibbon and, as Mrs. Bates adds, "twenty or thirty yards of Scott" and "enough Encyclopaedia Britannica to reach around the corner and back again" (*WP* 47, 49, 50).

Bates's house certainly grabs the attention of Jane Marshall throughout the show of the house during her first visit. Surprised and impressed, Jane cannot help ejaculating her comment when she sees a big table with a "shining inkstand" and an "immaculate blotting-pad": "What a grand table to sit and write papers at!" Mrs. Bates's response only adds more to her surprise:

> "But, really, I don't suppose I've written two lines at that table since it was put there. And as for all these books, Heaven only knows where the keys are to get at them with. I can't do anything with them; why, some of them weigh five or six pounds." (*WP* 50)

Mrs. Bates's remarks here sound like a complaint: the difficulty of locating the keys and the excessive weight of the books. Yet, this very complaint in fact carries a subtle message, which is meant to refute Jane's effort to underline the practical function and use value of all these objects on display. Jane seems to have perceived the purpose of these objects instantly when she mutters, "All for show and display" (*WP* 50).

However, Jane does not understand the value of "show" for attention here. She only mutters, "[B]ought by the pound and stacked by the cord; doing nobody any good—their owners least of all" (*WP* 50). Mrs. Bates, who gets no music out of her piano, no reading out of her books, and no sleep out of her bed, seems "a strange woman" to Jane. Mrs. Bates's "ostentatious pride" probably appears as ridiculous as what Winthrop Floyd has observed in his brother Walworth Floyd's peculiar concern with his shoes, "a neglect of the head in favor of the toe" (*WP* 51, 59; *CD* 141). Bates's conspicuous display seems like an unnecessary "waste."

"Waste," a term that Veblen has also used in his discussion of the leisure class, is a precise verdict on the phenomenon of attention. However, the term is used in Veblen's discussion as a technical one which implies "no deprecation of the motives."[48] "Waste" is not an "illegitimate expenditure" of human product or of human life; instead, it is just as legitimate as any other expenditure. To put it another way, "waste" is a form of meaningful expenditure that gives the user a superior material feature or striking aura to win public attention and to gain increasing social value. For example, women's dress—the high heel, the skirt, the impracticable bonnet, and the corset—and even the discomfort of the actual wearing may appear impractical or unnecessary. Yet the very impracticality, or "waste," is indicative of the wearer's independence from manual productive activity and her position in socioeconomic life.[49]

Hence, the "waste" in the novel is not equal to waste. It is an expenditure, calculated for an ultimate gaining through convincing the public of the social value and financial status of the "spendthrift." Mr. and Mrs. Bates have been conscious of the importance of material display ever since their marriage years ago. They deliberately chose to get married at "the most fashionable church in town" because their neighbors—those "Terrace Row people"—were all stylish. The young couple then decided to give a good show to the big people there and to impress them with extravagance. With this expensive beginning and a good show, the Bateses march "right up the front steps" and soon become a leading part of the community (*WP* 53).

Manners, like the ostentatious material display, equally serve to attract attention. In Fuller's novels, admirable manners, as shown in decorum, good taste, education, and self-improvement, are employed as assertions of special excellence and individual value. Manners are not exactly dollars; yet they are acquired and maintained on a considerable economic basis, and they are thus as real as dollars. For this reason, displaying good manners carries exactly the same effect as displaying material possessions.

Mrs. Bates, whose manners instantaneously distinguish her from many of the characters in both of these novels, is a beautiful example. She is a master of rhetoric: knowing when to use "a low, quiet tone" for a surprisingly thundering strike or when to use circumlocution in order to become most effective. She knows "what tone to take" on a certain occasion to achieve the best effect. She can be profoundly formal and punctilious; she can also put on an air of the "most elaborate and ingenious simplicity," as exemplified in her arranging Rosy's debut party (*WP* 102, 107). Her skill of persuasion is accompanied by a tactfully exquisite manner: with "sympathetic persistence," she makes Mrs. Marshall believe that she is deeply interested; she then adopts an "innocent, left-handed fashion" to instruct the latter without causing her to betray "social ignorance"; finally, she allays Mrs. Marshall's timidity by making such a serious social event appear to be "a mere bagatelle for simplicity and informality" (*WP* 102-03). She is capable of steering the course of conversation without any overt sign of dominance, and she can draw all her followers' attention without a coercive command.

Education offers intellectual enrichment, but receiving an education does not necessarily mean seeking intellectual development. Being a pupil may simply aim to put on an ostentatious show. Mrs. Bates receives music education as Jane does, but she does not intend to learn music or be a musician. Her present status of being a pupil in a music class is meant to signify "a conspicuous exemption" from all useful employment and productive labor.[50] Her present financial possessions enable her to be free from any productive labor or, to put it another way, to take leisure as her self-employment. Like other leisure-class members who brag of their quasi-scholarly or quasi-artistic accomplishments, Mrs. Bates is engaged in and enjoying, in Veblen's terms, the "unproductive expenditure of time."[51] Nevertheless, Mrs. Bates appears controlled and even self-criticizing in her remarks to Jane: "You were surprised, I saw, about my music-lessons: It *is* a little singular, I admit—my beginning as a teacher and ending as a pupil" (*WP* 52). Mrs. Bates then goes on to tell Jane that she herself was raised in a working class family in a small town. Her father was a carpenter, and she helped her mother do errands. She became a teacher at eighteen in order to earn her own bread, and she taught a class in a church basement. Mrs. Bates seems certainly more than "a little singular" since she is so candid in revealing her poor family background to Jane, with whom she has just become acquainted. Yet her deceptively frank revelation, which is set in the middle of the ostentatious display of her wealth, has a dramatic effect and engages more of Jane's attention to the Bates family's success.[52] And her "self-criticism" of "beginning as a teacher and ending as a pupil" is nothing but witty braggadocio.

Cornelia McNabb in *The Cliff-Dwellers* quickly comprehends the value of manners. She discerns that manners, as a code of status, are external features of some intrinsic attributes and personal value, and they are incompatible with vulgarity and productive labor. Good manners, manifesting themselves through decorum or education, are thus a means to distinguish the person from the commonplace. Cornelia, with an ambition to become a future Mrs. Bates or even Mrs. Ingles, thus spares no pain in improving her skills and decorum in her struggle for attention and social climbing. She takes a shorthand and typewriting class, and absorbs instructions, regarding speech, protocol, and norm from the leisure class around her.

Showing manners differs from material display in that the former is often abstract and intangible. Material possessions, being a skyscraper or a luxurious mansion, can be valued in monetary terms. Elegant decorum or behavior, however, resists such a calculation though it elicits one's admiration, similar to that of the material possessions. It may seem strange that physical body may sometimes become a part of the decorum. Cornelia, when discussing her ambition, tells George Ogden, ". . . I'm going to keep my hands as nice as I can; a girl never knows what she may have a chance to become. I don't imagine it will disfigure me much to run a typewriter" (*CD* 70). Cornelia's special care for her hands is neither an insane obsession nor a whim to avoid manual labor. She intends to preserve the suppleness and softness of her hands. The dexterity is not appreciated—or, at least, not important—since it is a mark of engagement in the manual labor. Suppleness and softness, on the other hand, indicate aloofness from demeaning productive activities, and her hands are thus for physical display. Similar physical display is also presented in the case of Floyd, whose hands are highlighted:

> [Floyd's] plump hands, by reason of the fine texture of the skin and the shapeliness of the nails, form a point that is distinctly aristocratic. Yet penmanship, under his manipulations, becomes a very crabbed and laborious affair, and this light species of manual labor is usually performed, so far as he is concerned, by other hands. (*CD* 9)

Floyd is also accustomed to worrying his head "about as few things as possible," and he has employed somebody else to do "his thinking" for him. His hands and head, disengaged from their normal functions, become a component of Floyd's manners. Together with the material possessions, such as the decorative electrical devices on the walls in his office, they purport to gain public attention, and stress Floyd's superior value, his leisure, and his distinction from the commonality.

Attention-seeking, which entails pecuniary emulation and invidious comparison,[53] is essentially relentless and throat-cutting. Economy of attention bears traces of primitive tribal societies. According to Veblen, in the predatory social economy, the function of the able-bodied man was to kill and destroy all competitors, and to reduce to subservience all alien forces in the environment that asserted themselves refractorily against his self-seeking interests. Slaughter was honorific and of high value, and acts of aggression were highly recognized.[54] In modern society, which is more peaceful than the primitive stage, the residue of the past is deposited. The residue of the past reveals itself in the desire for attention, which results in fierce competition and transforms the competitors into predators.

Fuller's novels unveil the fierce and dehumanizing competition for attention in this economy. The competitive world is cruel and ruthless. The advancement of Rosy is structured on the very depreciation of the socially disadvantaged. At her debut party, Rosy, "the leading luminary of the day," gains attention and is transformed into a social celebrity. Being happy and victorious, she "shifted any embarrassment incident to the occasion from her own shoulder to those of her mother's friends—two or three of whom, retired and aging persons, withdrew feeling their own social rustiness quite keenly" (*WP* 106-07). Economy of attention can be violent since it is embellished with military terms and perturbed by striking clangs. A dinner party in a most gentle milieu, such as Bates's house, becomes a battle ground for display and attention. Mrs. Bates, who invites the Marshalls for dinner, arranges to banish "all traces of social warpaint" by dispensing with most male servants and having the remaining servants dressed in plainest liveries. Mrs. Bates intends to make the Marshalls feel on "a peace footing." But this "little" or "plainest" dinner at a great power's house turns out to be a battle of competition. Granger Bates's conversation sounds like "lumbering charges" of a "cavalry," and his wife exacts Marshall's attention for her luxurious dormitory plan (*WP*

159, 160). Mrs. Bates even "demands" Mrs. Marshall to give attention to her bragging about her son Billy Bates (*WP* 160). Marshall, mortified and humiliated, resembles a military leader suffering from a crushing defeat. He has "never felt smaller" and is even ashamed to look up (*WP* 162).

Attention-seeking, as a mechanism, shapes and reshapes social structure. It changes the distances among human beings, and advances or demotes them on the social ladder. Fuller presents these changes in the social grid through his characters who exert their nervous and tense efforts for social climbing. These characters may be divided into four general categories: the newcomers, the new immigrants, the family members, and the money class.

Fuller shows that big cities have become powerful magnets attracting thousands of newcomers from across the country. A social grid of intricate relations is formulated, and people are either closely or remotely chained and connected. People from all regions of the country and all social levels stream into big cities and work in the skyscrapers, where social life and business life are fused, or they gather in department stores or outside on the street. The city generously lifts the veil and reveals elegance, glamor, and extravaganza of the money class for new immigrants to admire, contemplate, and emulate. In his study of nineteenth-century Chicago, Hugh Dalziel Duncan points out that "window shopping" became Chicago's "city habit" and tempted the young Chicagoans to scrutinize the mystery and wonder of the wealth, which appeared wonderfully close at hand.[55] Social classes seemed diminished, and all were chained together. In *The Cliff-Dwellers*, Anne Wilde, Floyd's sister-in-law, needs a business adviser, and George Ogden offers to introduce Eugene McDowell, who is engaged to his sister. Fuller then delineate the winding, lengthy social "chain": Wilde suddenly "found herself so near to the future husband of the sister of the man who had just presented a letter of introduction to her own brother-in-law" (*CD* 30).

The social grid, different from the constant and solid geographical formation, is elastic and mutable. Cornelia, a newcomer from Wisconsin, successfully catches the eye and then wins the heart of Burt Brainard, the eldest son of the millionaire banker Erastus Brainard, and she is elevated to increasingly conspicuous positions. Cornelia begins to imitate the wealthy and elegant Mr. Floyd, and adopts the fashionable irregular use of slang words (*CD* 190). As soon as her marriage with Burt is celebrated in print, she sets out to plan a new house for $70,000 near the waterworks tower to bang her shield "against the shields of other amazons" (*CD* 225-26). Similarly, Jane is embraced by Mrs. Bates as "one of *us*" no sooner than the latter has recognized that Jane is her dear friend's daughter. Yet a seemingly short distance in the social grid, on the other hand, can be elongated infinitely. The Beldens, from a small town in Massachusetts, live only three hundred feet across the street from Mrs. Bates, but they find themselves "three hundred miles" away from "the stubborn little clique" (*WP* 65, 101, 102). For the same reason, attending an exclusive game-dinner at the Pacific becomes an indication of winning attention and enviable social prestige. And failure to receive an invitation to the game-dinner party could be an alarming signal that one has been "dropped" out, and one's connection with the great and complex city is severed (*WP* 36, 37).

McDowell's case also proves that the social grid can be both rigid and flexible depending on the attention received. McDowell, a detestable selfish character, senses that getting Ingles's attention would bring him instant profit both financially and socially. He deliberately chooses Room 1262 as his office, not for better light or ventilation but for being next to Arthur Ingles's office in Room 1263. Between these two rooms is a door.

> This door was closed, but it was McDowell's dream and ambition to see it open. In his thoughts he constantly saw it standing ajar in an intimate and friendly fashion, while he and Ingles and other magnates of Ingles's ilk circulated through it freely and all did business together. (*CD* 100)

But the door has never been opened. Ingles, a social elite, deliberately poses an obscure profile like his plain name plate in very small letters on his office door. Yet the inconspicuousness makes the owner of the building mysterious and all the more compelling. McDowell is willing to give a full commitment for anything in order to get close to Ingles. He gets into St. Asaph's Church and assumes financial administration of its choir just because he may thus become acquainted with the men of wealth and power, including Arthur Ingles. But Ingles is present at the business meeting for no more than ten minutes and allows no chance for McDowell to get close to him. McDowell, a most imaginative person, tries to make an unprofitable land transaction with Ingles later simply for the profit of entering the mysterious door between 1262 and 1263, but Ingles rejects the offer with "a faintly cynical contempt" (*CD* 170). Despite McDowell's numerous attempts, Ingles commands his resignation of financial responsibility for the church choir:

> The communication might have been made by Ingles personally, or it might have been sent by his office-boy, or it might even (as a physical possibility) have been pushed in under the crack of the door between them. As a matter of fact, it came through the mail. So formal a transmission of so formidable a communication was conclusive; McDowell felt at once that all possibility of personal relations between himself and Ingles was at an end—that door in the wall between them was as good as bricked up. (*CD* 212-13)

In this economy of attention, little attention is given to the incompetent and the weaklings. The fierce competition for attention in the social grid neglects and discards a large part of society, especially the socially and economically disadvantaged, such as new immigrants, mostly from Eastern and Southern European countries. Briefly, yet disturbingly, Fuller introduces the fact that these new immigrants have become part of the city life and the cause of much social disorder and chaos.[56]

New immigrants are repelled and detested. The Van Horns and the Leppins are regarded as "steerage-rats" and the cause of much disturbance to the neighborhood. They are named "savages and hoodlums" (*WP* 133, 164). The wealthy avoid these culturally anonymous and unidentifiable new immigrants because to mix with them in the public sphere is detestable and "horrid" (*WP* 111). Socially and economically, skyscrapers are not for these immigrants, whose business is allowed to be conducted only "on the premises" or in their "burrow" (*WP* 134). Yet the bewildering strangeness of these new immigrants obstinately exhibits itself in the public arena. During Ogden's first few weeks in Chicago, he has encountered "a range of human types completely unknown to his past experience." Their "skulls, foreheads, gaits, odors, facial angles," as well as their eyes, ears, and hair, disorientingly confusing, elicit Ogden's curious scrutiny and philosophical contemplation. But he soon discovers that it is impossible to categorize these ethnic groups. One afternoon, when there is a heavy storm outside, Ogden in the public library at City Hall witnesses "the bogs of Kilkenny, the dung-heaps of the Black Forest, the miry ways of Transylvania and Little Russia" which have all "contributed" to the boisterous confusion inside. The scene astounds Ogden "with a sudden and sickening surprise" (*CD* 54-55).

These new immigrants also demand social recognition and call for the attention they have been denied. Instead of being suave or ostentatious materially, they resort to violence and constitute a potentially dangerous threat to society. They trample the sacred law and encroach upon their law-abiding neighbors' property. They break into the Marshalls' stable, damage the coach, and beat the coachman (*WP* 164). Yet, it is hard to put any of these law breakers in jail since the police and the ward alderman are their allies. The law seems incapable of exercising any punitive power over those criminals. Through Marshall and Roger, Fuller lifts "the cover" and shows that deep inside is "a hell-broth—thieves, gamblers, prostitutes, pawnbrokers, saloon-keepers, aldermen, heelers, justices, bailiffs, policemen. . . ." All these, as the enraged Roger Marshall explains, have been "concocted" within two decades with the influx of immigrants (*WP* 194-95).

Struggles for attention also find their way in families. The competition erodes family relationships and eventuates in family duels and even patricide, which have become common occurrences. Because of the competition, family relationships have been transformed into purely business relationships, and those who show no potential in bringing profit are often denied attention. J. Russell Vibert, a church choir and ordinary office clerk, marries Mary Brainard, but he enjoys no recognition from the family. Vibert complains indignantly that Erastus Brainard does not give him "any show," though he is Brainard's "son" (*CD* 150). Marcus Brainard, the second son of the family, is an artist type. He is also denied any chance to "show" since he has not even slight interest in business. He is shut out in the dark, dishevelled and deprived of all attention (*CD* 150, 262-70). He can appear only at night in the park of "forbidding bareness," and in the "ghastly illumination" of the arc-lights (*CD* 263). Being deprived of attention, Marcus loses his chance of gaining money from his father while his brother Burt acquires half a million. Marcus eventually kills his father in Brainard's own business office. In his depiction of this angry ousted son, Fuller again projects a close-up view of the hand, this time Marcus's: "His fingers felt thin and claw-like, and there was a grime rubbed into their cracked and roughened skin—those girlish fingers (his mother's fingers) that had once held a pencil so delicately" (*CD* 267). The emphasis here is clearly on the dehumanizing aspect of the family relation rather than Marcus's shabbiness. Fuller is pinpointing the continuation of the predatory nature in the modern world by contrasting softness ("girlish fingers") with roughness ("cracked and roughened"), and cultural demeanor ("held a pencil") with beastly frenzy ("claw-like").

Fuller's novels are thus full of frightfully intense anxiety under their apparent merriment. Thousands of nervous, restless souls spread out everywhere in the city, behind the "glittering" windows, against the glamorous decorations of the Clifton, and amid the civilized procession. Weaklings soon become martyrs and victims of the competition. Nevertheless, the success is similarly in varying degrees of nervous anxiety. Success and glory in the past do not guarantee eternal security. If these survivors do not proceed and adapt to the new environment, they will fade out of the picture shortly. Erastus Brainard and David Marshall, the successful captains of industry in these novels, are typical examples as they are nervously confronted with a vehement torrent of changing style of consumer culture and demand for more ostentatious display.

Brainard is a money machine, and his business success has made him a millionaire. The modern economy of attention is clearly incompatible with his life philosophy. The sole aim in his life is business. He enjoys no diversion, and the affairs of the Underground and his other companies continue to occupy "his attention" (*CD* 38).

> He had never eaten and drunk for anything but business—his family shared his farm-like fare and his primitive hours. He had never built for anything but business; though constantly investing in grounds and buildings, he had occupied his own home for fifteen years as a tenant merely, before he could bring himself to a grudging purchase. He never dressed for anything but business—he had never worn a dress-coat in his life. He wrote about nothing but business—his nearest relative was never more than "dear sir," and he himself was never more than "yours truly"; and he wrote on business letterheads even to his family. (*CD* 43-44)

His obsession with money transforms all social and familial relations into business relations.

Fuller's depiction of Brainard is both condemning and sympathetic. Brainard is unquestionably cruel and tricky, dedicated to gaining personal advantage for profit in predatory economic activities. He is forever a knife, ready to open and explore the "oyster," be it the community or his own wife (*CD* 39, 135). Nevertheless, Brainard, who symbolizes the conventional mode of financial manipulation prior to the 1880s, seems to be pitiably tortured by the new mode and gradually fading out of the picture. The economic mode is shifting more and more toward one in which "public recognition and acclaim" and "personalities" become the measurements of achievements.[57] It is a new mode, in which ostentatious waste is mandatory, and conspicuous consumption has replaced simple, though often tricky, manipulation. Along with the change appear the new definition of "competence" and the unprecedented "absentee ownership."[58] The Brainards' brownstone house in West Side is now overshadowed by the Ingleses' Clifton building and other adjacent buildings. Brainard suddenly recognizes the potential threat to his future success and even survival. But he is not willing to, or rather not able to, make a change. He flatly refuses to consider Fanny Valentine's suggestion to move his "benighted family" to the fashionable North Side. He exclaims, "I wouldn't live anywhere else if you paid me to. What's better than this?" (*CD* 138). In consequence, Brainard gradually recedes to assume a subordinate side role and may completely lose his position eventually.

David Marshall, an old settler in *With the Procession*, shares some similar traits and similar anxiety, though he is not as greedy and detestable as Brainard. Like the latter, Marshall is a man for business. He feels pleased and proud to furnish grocery supplies to the community and regards the business as a means for him to become "a useful, stable, honored member of society" (*WP* 21). But his inclination for steadiness becomes the very cause of his "falling, falling, falling behind" (*WP* 33). The family has been staying in the same neighborhood, now infiltrated by business and tenements, over the last thirty years while their old friends have all gradually moved away. They keep a carpet for fifteen years while at Riverdale no carpet is over fifteen months old. The Marshalls are no longer "prominent citizens" (*WP* 33). They have descended to become merely a geologic survival in the new age of ostentation.

Fuller stresses a massive, tyrannical encroachment of business and industrialism upon the Marshalls and their residence.[59] At the beginning of the novel, Fuller implies that the Marshalls have already been intimidated by "the threatening and evil actuality" of the great Black City (*WP* 10). The Chicago of the 1860s is retained as a memory of "an Arcadia" contrasted with the social reality two decades later. Soon violent blows begin to pound the family incessantly: the strike of the policeman; the advance of big hotels and towering walls that shut out the sunlight and bring deafening noises; the transformation of a quiet neighborhood into a Babel, boisterous, filthy, and heterogeneous (*WP* 10, 20, 21). Most devastating of all is the Marshalls' case against their poor immigrant neighbor Van Horn, whose power has infiltrated into the legal system (*WP* 133-34, 163-64). The Marshalls are in panic since their private sector has been transgressed by industrialism and violence. Their once beautiful garden is withered, and their currant bushes and cherry trees have died out. Their property is broken into and damaged.

It is doubly difficult for Marshall to change his spending style and adapt to the mode of conspicuous waste. First, Marshall has never acquired "the useful and agreeable art of spending money" (*WP* 238). He is a thrifty, conservative entrepreneur, to whom profit means a substantial return from an investment. He detests philanthropists such as Ingles and defines philanthropy as a "current fad." Even though he loves to please his wife, he would not resort to an ostentatious manner like Ingles (*WP* 244). Unfortunately, situations are beginning to be different from what they used to be. One needs to find means to have people "*see*," such as by building a permanent, solid structure, with names carved in gray-stone over the doorway (*WP* 95). Now conspicuous waste is an art of saving, and philanthropic "giving" becomes a means to bring credit, attain a reputation, and gain attention. However, Marshall finds it incongruous with his nature to cultivate "the art of giving" and to win attention through waste.

The second difficulty that confronts Marshall is related to the disturbing immigrants such as the Van Horns and the Leppins. Marshall's contemplation of donating his property brings out a complicated issue: the relation of accumulation of wealth to democracy. To Marshall, the art of giving seems a revolutionary practice: in order to win public attention and be a victor, he should be willingly deprecated by "an alien and rabble populace" (*WP* 243). But to give out his hard earned money to the public seems unacceptable to him. Pain and anxiety grind Marshall's heart as this out-moded entrepreneur is unable to adapt himself to the art of giving.

The two novels, concerned with the socioeconomic phenomenon of attention-seeking, express a moral vision through their formal development. Fuller, who shows a deep interest in realism, expounds his theory of the novel in a posthumously published essay, "Howells or James?" (written in 1885).[60] In the essay, Fuller acknowledges that both James and Howells are talented and accomplished writers. Nevertheless, Howells is "a realist" while James is only "an idealist." Howells understands that writers should take a great interest in "the common level of general humanity" in this modern and democratic society. He regards realism as a way to show "a phase of humanity." Dedicated to treating "plain every day [sic] people and plain every day [sic] happiness," Howells is cultivating the "field of sympathetic realism." While James considers life as "a superficies" and distances himself from it, Howells regards life as "a substance" and holds a sympathetic attitude toward life. To Fuller, Howells's realism is thus "much more healthy and vigorous" than James's.[61]

In the same essay, Fuller elucidates the new function of the novel in this demographically and economically changing society: "new theories in philosophy, new ideas in art, new phases in religion, politics, and what not" have all been included in the novel. The novel, Fuller remarks, starts to play the role of "the great universal medium." He points out that a realistic novel provides sociological studies, and the pages of *Atlantic* and the *Century* provide the record and study of "the formulation of American society."[62] Fuller clearly sets two measuring standards for the novel by prioritizing its sociological functions: one, a true depiction of all aspects of contemporary daily life; two, a social and moral fulfillment. Again Howells is cited as better accomplished and more favorable since he follows the pulse of the nation, takes the daily socioeconomic activities as his subject, and treats his characters honestly and sympathetically. With this "intimation," Howells is able to present a "design to bring order out of . . . social chaos."[63]

The two measuring standards set by Fuller—a true depiction and a moral fulfillment—are the very equivalent phrases of the dual nature of a realistic novel: mimetic (or posterior) in its relation to the past social experience, and corrective (or premonitory) to the future. With this dual nature, Fuller's novels, like Howells's and all other realistic novels, are always socially and economically engaged. As a "sociologist" and as an admirer of Howells, Fuller takes contemporary Chicago as the locus of his novels and the phenomenon of attention as the subject. At the same time, Fuller makes a subtle moral point in his selection and arrangement of details.[64] By writing realistic novels, Fuller purports to offer his "design to bring order out of . . . social chaos."[65]

The dual nature may be further illustrated with the word "story" Fuller uses in his introduction of the Clifton at the beginning of *The Cliff-Dwellers*. Fuller, in a bitter tone, maps out the contemporary Chicago as a primitive landscape, which undergoes construction and corrosion simultaneously. Fuller then writes,

> Means have been found to measure its progress—just as a scale has been arranged to measure the rising of the Nile or to gauge the draught of an ocean liner. In this case the unit of measurement is called the "story." (*CD* 2)

The word "story" is apparently used as a pun. Each "story" (as "floor") of the skyscraper certainly supplies excellent materials and details for a realistic novel and an accurate measurement of material construction.[66] In the meantime, the word "story" (as "narrative") may refer to a realistic novel, functioning as a measurement of social progress, a guidance, and a mentor.[67] The first meaning is directed at the mimetic aspect of realism; the second suggests the social function of the fiction.

Fuller's novels, while presenting the phenomenon of attention, offer him a venue to voice his concern through a moral design for a new economy. The formal development of the novel allows Fuller to present the design without overtly intervening or being subjective. Fuller's novels provide him with an opportunity to reconstruct social reality to extirpate the moral and civic evil through an intriguing formal construction, particularly the marriage, without prescribing explicitly a dose for the social problems.

It can be meaningful and revealing to compare the marriages in these two novels and recognize some similarities and differences. In "My Early Books," Fuller recalls the writing of *The Cliff-Dwellers* and mentioned that the crucial question he raised in the novel was whether or not the marriage choice was an individual issue. "Since then," Fuller writes, "I have tried to intimate the theme plainly, on the first page, if not in the title."[68] Both novels have the marriage of the wealthy patriarch's daughter: the marriage of Abbie to Ogden, and that of Jane to Brower. Even though Ogden marries twice, and Bower marries only once, there are two major, informing similarities between these marriages. First, both Jessie Bradley and the former Jane Marshall actively emulate and follow the fashion. In *The Cliff-Dwellers*, Jessie, Ogden's first, ill-chosen wife, is a pursuer and victim of conspicuous consumption. Jessie likes "circulation" and wants to "circulate" (*CD* 86). She is motivated by an unquenchable desire for pecuniary emulation: worshipping names of the public figures; entertaining extravagantly the social celebrities; enjoying display; cultivating a "ravenous taste" for superfluous luxury to emulate, to show, to waste, and to compete with Cecilia Ingles or other social elite (*CD* 218-31, 246-55). Soon after the wedding, Ogden realizes the difference between Jessie and her parents, whose conventional modest life-style has played a decisive role in his marriage choice. Ogden finds himself incapable of handling Jessie and her increasingly luxurious spending style, a situation foreshadowed by the horse wagon trip from the station before their marriage.

> She rushed him through the outskirts of the town; she bumped over the cumbrous plank crossings, she grazed one or two of the wooden posts that held up oil-lamps, she charged a flock on its homeward way from church and cut it into two frightened and indignant halves. She was on her native heath; she felt it; she showed it. (*CD* 177)

Jessie's extravagant waste leads to her own fatal illness after the death of her infant son, and Ogden is consequently dragged into debt. Jessie's death, as Pilkington noted, forms "a pathetic ending to a marriage already doomed by the competition for social recognition in Chicago."[69]

Jane Marshall in the first half of *With the Procession* is also on the showy path of social emulation. Jane's family role is almost as important as Abbie's in keeping her family "from disintegration" (*WP* 32). After her acquaintance with Mrs. Bates, Jane becomes Mrs. Bates's "unconscious pupil," and Bates her "godmother," "preceptress," and "monitress" (*WP* 120, 122, 123). Mrs. Bates teaches Jane how to improve physical glamour and how to cultivate an extravagant consuming style. "You'd better have this," Mrs. Bates would thus instruct Jane. "It becomes you first-rate—

you won't find anything nicer" (*WP* 123). She shows Jane that an exorbitant price can elevate the value of the consumer. A couple of months of intense study transforms Jane into a presentable girl, appearing in the theatre next to Mrs. Bates in her box.

Second, the couples in both Ogden's second marriage and Brower's marriage make conscious effort to distance themselves from ostentatious display. In *The Cliff-Dwellers*, Ogden finally chooses to marry Abbie, who is "a quiet, self-poised girl" with "a pair of cool, steady grey eyes." She seems "wholesome, stable, capable of keeping herself well in hand" (*CD* 57-58). Abbie always maintains "her own essence" and keeps a clear perception of reality. She is forgiving and, after her father's death, readily accepts the repentant Ogden as he is. Ogden, with a cautious nature, appreciates Abbie's intrinsic qualities, such as "resolution," "courage," "tenderness and fidelity" (*CD* 320). Their marriage involves "no social celebration," and they live "in the same house" where Ogden used to live. (*CD* 322).

Jane in *With the Procession* eventually turns away from her pursuit of ostentatious display. She will not have social entertainment and does not want to seek attention. She even rejects the idea of entertaining Susan Bates and Cecilia Ingles, a practice that she now calls "picnic business" and "all nonsense" (*WP* 180). Through a sketch of Jane at the talk with the architect Tom Bingham, Fuller shows a change in Jane. Even though Mrs. Bates's influence of extravagant display is still traceable there, the ornamental quality is somewhat being contrasted, diluted, and absorbed by an essentially antithetical quality.

> Jane stood there on the foundations, clad in the ample and voluminous fashion of the day and topped off with a distinctly stylish hat. She has had a long regimen of fencing and dumbbells, and her self-imposed superintendence of the new house had led to many hours spent in the open air. Her hair was blowing airily about her face. . . . (*WP* 209-10)

Production and independence ("self-imposed superintendence"), natural exertion ("in the open air"), and unaffectedness (dishevelled hair)—these details, opposed to conspicuous showiness and extravagant waste, indicate a change in Jane. Later she reproaches herself remorsefully that she is "to blame" for all the disastrous consequences that she has brought to the family by building "a nice house" (*WP* 261). She comes to realize that the world of fashion, with conspicuous material display, is "empty," "cold," and "unsympathetic" (*WP* 263).

Brower, the man Jane marries, is the "ethical center in the novel."[70] He is "earnest" and "serious" (*WP* 125). He objects to money orientation and a conspicuous life-style. He wants to live "inconspicuously," and he does not even have a dress-coat, for he thinks that it is "ugly and foolish" (*WP* 125).

Brower's radical political view makes him an unyielding fighter against fashion and an advocate for the care of the socially and economically disadvantaged. As a member of the Consolation Club, Brower participates in a critical discourse commenting on and contending the social changes in the last twenty years since the centennial celebration in Philadelphia in 1876 and the railroad riots in 1877. Brower shows an understanding of and sympathy toward immigrants, and he calls for democracy to counterattack feudalism. Rather than praising the city as a source of money-making, he exposes the disturbing consequences of attention-seeking: everyone "cultivates his own little bed," and no one cares about "the paths between," which are covered with "the weeds of a rank iniquity" (*WP* 203).

To correct social problems, Brower calls for an interest in the general good, and a concern with the dispossessed.

> "They want care and attention—as the doctors say; they need a law-dispensary—that's about it. There are institutions that look after people's minds and bodies gratis; I want to see an institution started up that will do as much for their estates. I want to see a building for it, with an endowment and a library and a force of practitioners. To think of all the things that a man with money and ideas and sympathies might do—and should do—in a town like this!" (*WP* 204)

Brower's aspiration differs fundamentally from those of Ingles, Bates, Marshall, and Rosy in its aiming to *give* attention rather than *seek* attention, and to bring about economic equality and social order rather than to become a social predator.

Brower stands as a contrast to Tom Bingham, Jane's most passionate suitor. Bingham is a fashionable architect, who abides by Chicago's "civic building fad." He bolsters fashion and attention-seeking,

> "The man who makes his mark here to-day will enjoy a fame which will spread as the fame of the city spreads and its power and prosperity

> increases. You know what we are destined to be—a hundred times greater than we are to-day. Fasten your name on the town, and your name will grow as the town itself does." (*WP* 162-63)

By having Jane accept Brower's proposal, Fuller both rejects Bingham's ideas and confirms Brower's viewpoints, that is, Chicago's mad rush toward attention and material display is perverse, and new institutions should be anticipated to serve the public interest.

Hence, by ending his novels with these marriages, Fuller suggests a moral design for a curb on the current phenomenon of attention-seeking.[71] The two couples will lead a comfortable life against the trend for attention and ostentatious display. Both Abbie and Jane are not interested in hunting for attention, and Ogden and Brower do not have demanding wives to satisfy. Moreover, both Abbie and Jane are financially secure. And all four of them have a "taste" for a modest life-style as opposed to the vulgar money fetishism; yet they are practical and realistic, ready to enrich themselves with hard work.

Nevertheless, these endings bear traces of authorial arbitrariness due to Fuller's moral intention. One such example is the death of the elderly fathers. Ogden and Brower at first believe that marriage "concerns only the two people primarily involved" (*CD* 78). The belief is soon proven wrong by Ogden's first marriage experience. Marriage, as Fuller once remarked, is "less a matter between individuals than between families."[72] It is because of the disreputable Brainard that Ogden gives up Abbie and chooses to marry Jessie (*CD* 204-07). Ogden, who later realizes his mistake, is unable to go back precisely because of the tyrannous Brainard, whose existence makes his union with Abbie impossible (*CD* 320). Likewise, the presence of Marshall in *With the Procession* obstructs Brower from marrying Jane. Marshall wants Jane to marry a Westerner, a genuine Chicagoan, and one who has done "a little something" to make the city what it is. Only Bingham could best meet these criteria. Hence, while the deaths of Brainard and Marshall, to the community, are like the demise of "another old settler" and a reminder of the "humble beginnings" (*WP* 273), their disappearance signifies a breakthrough in the lives of these couples. With this utopian construct, Fuller recognizes the inevitable involvement of the family in the marriage and guarantees the attainment of a successful marriage. He seems to indicate that a painful mourning gives birth to the happy, ideal marriage of the young couple.

Even though Fuller is critical of this phenomenon of attention-seeking, he avoids being idealistic by placing these two young couples in the midst of social tension for attention. *With the Procession* ends with Jane's decision and Brower's acquiescence to put David Marshall's money into a collegiate building. And in *The Cliff-Dwellers*, Ogden and Abbie, though their wedding involves "no social celebration," go to a series of shows at the theatre luminous in ivory and gold. Fuller narrates that Ogden and Abbie "toned down their existence" among thousands of people there, yet they are situated among invidious comparisons. When Ingles appears at the theatre, enjoying absolute public attention, Cornelia swears ambitiously, "Just you wait. Burt's smart and I'm careful, and we shall catch up to you yet" (*CD* 323). Fuller concludes the novel with Ogden's response:

> He [Ogden] knew that she was Cecilia Ingles, and his heart was constricted by the sight of her. It is for such a woman that one man builds a Clifton and that a hundred others are martyred in it. (*CD* 324)

Recognizing and criticizing the economy of attention is a moral execution of the form of the novel, but this criticism can only be carried out with a feeling of inevitable involvement.

Notes

Introduction

1. Mark Twain, "The Revised Catechism," *New York Tribune*, Sept. 27, 1871: 6.

2. William Dean Howells, *The Rise of Silas Lapham* (Bloomington: Indiana UP, 1971) 64.

3. See Louis M. Hacker, *The Course of American Economic Growth and Development* (New York: Wiley, 1970); Alan Trachtenberg, *The Incorporation of America* (New York: Hill, 1982); and Robert H. Wiebe, *The Search for Order 1877-1920* (New York: Hill, 1967).

4. Walter F. Taylor uses the term "economic novels" to denominate most of the American novels of the period that showed an interest in economics. See Walter F. Taylor, *The Economic Novel in America* (Chapel Hill: U of North Carolina P, 1942).

5. Claude Reherd Flory, *Economic Criticism in American Fiction: 1792 to 1900* (Philadelphia, n.p., 1936) 13.

6. See Matthew Josephson, *The Robber Barons* (1934; New York: Harcourt, 1962); Peter d'A. Jones, ed. *The Robber Barons Revisited* (Boston: Heath, 1968); and Thomas B. Brewer, ed. *The Robber Barons: Saints or Sinners* (New York: Holt, 1970).

7. Jan W. Dietrichson, *The Image of Money* (New York: Humanities P, 1969) 378-80.

8. See Marc Shell, *The Economy of Literature* (Baltimore: Johns Hopkins UP, 1978) 1-10, and Marc Shell, *Money, Language and Thought* (Berkeley: U of California P, 1982).

9. Shell, *Economy* 1-10.

10. Shell, *Money* 4.

11. Shell, *Economy* 154.

12. Michael Gilmore, *American Romanticism and the Marketplace* (Chicago: U of Chicago P, 1985) 1.

13. Walter Benn Michaels, *The Gold Standard and the Logic of Naturalism* (Berkeley: U of California P, 1987).

14. See Wai-Chee Dimock, "Degrading Exchange: Edith Wharton's House of Mirth," *PMLA* 100 (1985) 783-92, and Wai-Chee Dimock, "The Economy of Pain: The Case of Howells," *Raritan* 9 (1990): 99-119. Rpt. as "The Economy of Pain: Capitalism, Humanitarianism, and the Realistic Novel," *New Essays on the Rise of*

Silas Lapham, ed. Donald Pease (Cambridge: Cambridge UP, 1991) 67-90.

15. Dimock, "Pain" 80.

16. Speculation soon after the Civil War became a nation-wide phenomenon. Hundreds and thousands of people were involved in financial "ventures." J. K. Medbery, an observer of 1870, reported, "Gold was the favorite with the ladies. Clergymen affected mining stock and petroleum. Lawyers had a penchant for Erie. Solid merchants preferring their customary staples, sold cotton or corn for future delivery or bought copper or salt on margin." Scc J. K. Medbery, *Men and Mysteries of Wall Street* (Osgood, 1870), qtd. in Josephson 152.

17. Thomas Nast, "Milk-Tickets for Babies, In Place of Milk," Cartoon, from David A. Wells, *Robinson Crusoe's Money* (New York: Harper, 1876) 97. Both Michaels and Shell give an interesting and insightful reference to the issue in their discussion of *McTeague* and "The Gold Bug." See Michaels 151-53, and Shell, *Money* 5-23.

18. See Frank Norris, *McTeague* (1899; New York: Norton, 1977) 72-73, 84, 135, 174-75.

19. William Dean Howells, *A Hazard of New Fortunes* (Bloomington: Indiana UP, 1976) 184.

20. In 1890, with the advancement of industrialization, seven-eighths of the families held only one-eighth of the national wealth while one percent of the families in America held more than ninety-nine percent of the remaining. See Charles B. Spahr, *An Essay on the Present Distribution of Wealth in the United States*, 2nd ed. (New York: Crowell, 1896) 69.

21. Henry George, *Progress and Poverty* (London: Kegan Paul, Trench and Co., 1883) 4.

22. Jacob Riis, *How The Other Half Lives* (New York: Scribner's, 1890) 109. See also Oscar Handlin's account of the immigrant history of the U.S. in his *The Uprooted* (New York: Grosset, 1951).

23. William Dean Howells, *A Traveller from Altruria* (1894; New York: Harper, 1908) 60-62, 87, 190.

24. Jean-Christopher Agnew, "A House of Fiction," in Simon J. Bronner, ed. *Consuming Visions* (New York: Norton, 1989) 137.

25. See Alfred Chandler, "The Beginnings of 'Big Business' in American Industry," *The Essential Chandler* (Boston: Harvard Business School P, 1988) 46-73. In his discussion of the big business in American industry, Chandler used the terms "combination" and "integration" in reference to the merger movement in the economic history near the turn of the century. Relevant to this is Chandler's study of the influence of railroad construction on managerial concepts and skills. See Alfred Chandler, *The Visible Hand: The Managerial Revolution in American Business* (Cambridge, MA: Belknap, 1977).

26. See Thorstein Veblen, *The Theory of the Leisure Class* (1899; New York: NAL, 1953).

27. See Thorstein Veblen, *The Theory of the Leisure Class* (1899; New York: NAL, 1953).

28. Eric J. Sundquist, *American Realism* (Baltimore: Johns Hopkins UP, 1982) 7.

29. Amy Kaplan, *The Social Construction of American Realism* (Chicago: U of Chicago P, 1988) 9.

30. Philip Fisher, *Hard Facts* (New York: Oxford UP, 1987) 8-9.

31. Horatio Alger's success stories, for example, simply provided wish fulfillment or, as John Tebbel commented, pleased "the fantasies of boys growing up in that time and place." See John Tebbel, *From Rags to Riches* (New York: Macmillan, 1963) 3-18. Also see Gary Scharnhorst, *The Lost Life of Horatio Alger, Jr.* (Bloomington, Indiana UP, 1985) 149-56.

Chapter I: Economy of Insanity

1. Mark Twain and Charles Dudley Warner, *The Gilded Age* (Hartford: American Publishing Co., 1873) 498. The novel is hereafter referred to by page number in the text.

2. Norman Dain, *Concepts of Insanity in the United States, 1785-1865* (New Brunswick, NJ: Rutgers UP, 1964) 88.

3. The term "psychiatry" was first cited in Joseph E. Worcester, *A Universal and Critical Dictionary of the English Dictionary* (1846), and the term "psychiatrist" was first used in *Century Dictionary* (1889-91). See *OED* (Oxford: Clarendon, 2nd ed., 1989). Though there is no evidence that "psychiatrist" was ever used as early as the 1840s and 1850s, for the sake of convenience I use this term here referring to the medical practitioners of psychiatry, a burgeoning area in medical science.

4. Dain 87.

5. Dain 91-92.

6. *OED*.

7. Andrew Dickson White, *A History of the Warfare of Science with Theology in Christendom*, vol. 2 (New York: Appleton, 1910) 130-34.

8.Thomas Maeder, *Crime and Madness* (New York: Harper, 1985) 38.

9. Louis E. Reik, "The Doe-Ray Correspondence," *The Yale Law Journal*, 63 (1953) 183.

10. Dr. Isaac Ray's work *Medical Jurisprudence of Insanity* (1838) influenced the making of the M'Naghten rules in 1843 in England. However, Ray did not agree with the M'Naghten rules, particularly the delusion rule, and his criticism of them was added to the third edition of his work in 1853. For his criticism, see Isaac Ray, *Treatise on the Medical Jurisprudence of Insanity*, 3rd ed. (Boston: Little, 1853) 43-50.

11. "Plea of Insanity in Criminal Cases," *Monthly Law Reporter* 10 (1847): 10, qtd. in

John Starrett Hughes, *In the Law's Darkness* (New York: Oceana P, 1986) 65. See also John Biggs, Jr., *The Guilty Mind* (Baltimore: Johns Hopkins UP, 1955) 100-01, 109, 117.

12. See Hughes 66.

13. Hughes 67.

14. See Maeder 40. In demonstrating the "foolish blindness brought about by too close reliance on imperfect verbal formulations," Ray cited the case of John Barclay, a young Scot, who could not "appreciate the difference between killing a human being and killing an ox." But he was convicted and executed simply because of his "vague awareness that both of these acts were somehow wrong."

15. Hughes 50.

16. See Maeder 47. It should be noted, however, that Ray had many supporters in the legal field as well, among whom the most prominent was New Hampshire Justice Charles Doe, whose New Hampshire Rules were essentially a silent acknowledgment and practice of Isaac Ray's theory. A good discussion of the famous Doe-Ray correspondence, consisting of about two dozen letters written in the late 1860s, is provided in Reik's study. See Reik 183-96.

17. See Maeder 43, 48 and 49.

18. Hughes 82.

19. Rex V. Creighton, 14 Can. Cr. Cas. 349 (Canada, 1908), qtd. in Maeder 49, n. 24.

20. See William Archibald Dunning, *Reconstruction Political and Economic 1865-1877* (New York: Harper and Brothers, 1907) 141-42.

21. Van Wyck Brooks, *The Ordeal of Mark Twain* (New York: Dutton, 1920; rev. 1933) 77.

22. To Samuel Johnson, speculation should be defined as follows: 1) Examination by the eye; view; 2) (An) examiner; (a) spy; 3) Mental view; intellectual examination; 4) A train of thoughts formed by meditation; 5) Mental scheme not reduced to practice; 6) Power of sight (not in use). See R. H. Mottram, *A History of Financial Speculation* (London: Chatto, 1929) 1-2.

23. Samuel Maunder, *Biographical Treasury* (1838), qtd. in Mottram 2.

24. Mottram 42.

25. Brooks 80.

26. Brooks 84.

27. Mark Twain, *Roughing It* (New York: NAL, 1962) 162.

28. David R. Sewell, *Mark Twain's Languages* (Berkeley: U of California P, 1987) 37.

29. Richard Grant White, *Words and Their Uses, Past and Present: A Study of the English Usage*, 20th ed. (Boston: Houghton, 1892) 80-81, qtd. in Sewell 44.

30. Sewell 44.

31. Kenneth Andrew interprets the novel as a "reactionary book," a view that I dis-

agree with. Truly, the characters depicted in the book are "ignorant" and many are even "stupid and self-seeking," but the authors' views are critical rather than "reactionary." Their belief and hope in the social progress is perceivable in the novel. By defining the novel as "reactionary," Andrew misses the ambivalence of the authors' attitude. See Kenneth Andrew, *Nook Farm* (Cambridge: Harvard UP, 1950) 184.

32. This is the term that Andrew has used to define Sellers. See Andrew 184-85.

33. Richard Sax, "Living in the Realm of Possibility," in *Mark Twain Journal* 21 (1983): 38-41.

34. Brooks argues that Americans after the Civil War needed to romanticize their situation and to propagate illusions or myths in order to "overcome hostile influences." See Brooks 86-88. In light of this, Sellers's rhetoric has played a paradoxically positive role.

35. William Adrian Bonger has a brief discussion of adultery in *Criminality and Economic Conditions* (Boston: Little, 1916). Bonger begins his discussion of adultery with citing the epigram that "the history of property is also that of theft," and he then argues that adultery, in a metaphorical sense, is an economic issue because human beings are "not monogamous by nature" and want to acquire some more extramarital relations. See Bonger, 609-11. Selby's bigamy with Laura, though seemingly a simple act of pure lust, is metaphorically an economic appropriation of youth, beauty, and sex. In addition, Braham's statement at the trial makes this economic relationship even more explicit in his emphasis on the financial status of Laura when Selby and Laura re-encounter years later: Laura's family have become "enormously rich by one of those sudden turns in fortune" (382).

36. This point could be further strengthened by the name of the New York hotel in which the murder takes place: "Southern." In the manuscript the hotel was named "Willard" at one point and was then changed to "Southern." See Bryant Morey French, *Mark Twain and the Gilded Age* (Dallas: Southern Methodist UP, 1965) 301, n. 7. The change itself seems suggestive: (1) The murder is the continuation of the historical duel between Laura and Selby, the two southerners; (2) It is a revenge in which the dead is a man and the former victimizer; (3) The locus of the "South" has moved northward, a sign indicating that the geographical division has been obliterated, and the new battle line has been formed based not on geography but on gender distinction.

37. Laura seems to have a capacity to create many choices and this very capacity makes her a source of economic turmoil and intolerable to the society. My point is just the opposite to that of Sewell, who states that "being wholly other-directed, she has no choice of her own." See Sewell 43.

38. Bryant Morey French has done a thorough study in this respect. His study shows that numerous characters, such as Dilworthy, Sellers, Hawkins, and Laura, as well as many events have their prototypes in real life, and they bear striking resemblance to these prototypes. See French, particularly 85-141.

39. See Everett Carter, *Howells and the Age of Realism* (Philadelphia: Lippincott,

1954) 73.

40. Mark Twain, "A New Crime," in *The Writings of Mark Twain*, (New York: Harper, 1906) xix: 244-50.

41. DaLancey Ferguson, "Mark Twain's Lost Curtain Speeches," *South Atlantic Quarterly*, xlii, qtd. in French 108.

42. Aristotle suggests that the writer is an economist who dispenses likenesses of impressions that he has received from nature. See Marc Shell, *The Economy of Literature* (Baltimore: Johns Hopkins UP, 1978) 104. In a sense, a novelist, in his "economic" activities, is more powerful and manipulative in determining the outcome of the trial than a judge or even Queen Victoria who decried the court's acquitting "insane" murderers, such as Oxford and M'Naghten, but had to leave the final decision to the judges. For a relevant discussion and Queen Victoria's letter dated March 12, 1843 in regard to the insanity defense trials, See Biggs 100-107.

43. Mark Twain, "To Mollie Fairbanks," 9 February 1876, *Mark Twain to Mrs. Fairbanks*, ed. Dixon Wector (San Marino, California: Huntington Library, 1949) 195.

44. In his letter to Mrs. Mary Mason Fairbanks, Mark Twain uses the term "*boss* chapter" referring to the climactic chapter of Laura's death. In the letter, Twain says that both Warner and Twain are offering a chapter for Livy Clemens and Susan Warner to judge and then choose one. In the postscript of the letter, it is added that "My climax chapter is the one accepted by Livy & Susie, & so my heroine, Laura, remains dead." See Trygve Thoreson, "Mark Twain's Unsentimental Heroine," in *The South Carolina Review* 14 (1982): 31-32.

45. Trygve Thoreson claims that Twain's reference to Laura's death in his letter to Fairbanks displays "a lack of seriousness." See Thoreson 31-32.

46. Justin Kaplan, *Mr. Clemens and Mark Twain* (New York: Simon, 1966) 95.

47. See Justin Kaplan, *Mark Twain and His World* (New York: Simon, 1974) 141-42.

48. This quotation is taken from Kaplan's book, and there is no page reference provided. See Kaplan 31.

49. Mark Twain, "Author's Preface to the London Edition," in Mark Twain and Charles Dudley Warner, *The Gilded Age*, 3 vols. (London: Routledge, 1874) 1: v.

50. Laura's killing of Selby, an insane act and a just retribution, is thus indicative of Twain's ambivalence toward the phenomenon of insanity.

Chapter II: Economy of Sympathy

1. William Dean Howells, *A Hazard of New Fortunes* (1890; Bloomington: Indiana UP, 1976) 61. The novel is hereafter referred to by page number in the text.

2. Max Scheler defines sympathy as ". . . feeling the other's feeling, not just knowing of it, nor judging that the other has it. . . ." Scheler points out that one does not go through the same experience in giving sympathy. "The other's feeling is given

exactly like a landscape which we 'see' subjectively in memory, or a melody which we 'hear' in similar fashion. . . . In the present case there is a real seeing or hearing, yet without the object seen or heard being perceived and accepted as really present; the past is simply 'represented'." Two other important points in Scheler's theory need to be noted here: (1) sympathy *presupposes* "some sort of *knowledge* of the fact, nature and quality of experience in other people;" (2) sympathy presupposes an awareness of the distance between the sympathizer and the object. See Peter Heath, trans., *The Nature of Sympathy*, by Max Scheler (1954; London: Routledge, 1970) 8-9, 22-23. Lauren Wispe's work, *The Psychology of Sympathy* (New York: Plenum, 1991), provides a comprehensive study of sympathy and a succinct summary of the theories of sympathy expounded by philosophers and scientists, such as David Hume, Adam Smith, Arthur Schopenhauer, and Charles Darwin.

3. Adam Smith, *The Theory of Moral Sentiments* (1759; Oxford: Clarendon, 1976) 43.

4. D. D. Raphael notes that Adam Smith uses the term "sympathy" in a special sense to mean "an imagined feeling in oneself" which would correspond with "an observed feeling in someone else." However, as Raphael points out, Smith's usage often slips back to the common one, that is, the actual experience of fellow-feeling with distress. D. D. Raphael, *Adam Smith* (Oxford: Oxford UP, 1985) 86. One of the major differences between these two types is the distance between the sympathizer and the object. This issue of distance will not be explored here since it is a complicated philosophical question and not critically relevant to the topic.

5. Smith 9.

6. Smith 24.

7. Smith 317.

8. Smith states in 1759 that "society may subsist among different men, as among different merchants, from a sense of its utility, without any mutual love or affection." See Smith, *Theory* 86. Smith's statement, with many other similar ones in his early work, seems much like the embryo of his emphasis on self-interest in *The Wealth of Nations*. However, there exists a key difference: lack of mutual love or affection in the former is just one of the conditions for the subsistence of human society; self-interest in the latter, on the other hand, carries a primary role in social and economic development.

9. Adam Smith, *The Wealth of Nations* (1776; New York: The Modern Library, 1965) 14.

10. Smith, *Wealth* 14.

11. In his discussion of Adam Smith's two works, D. D. Raphael argues that Smith is consistent in his points. Raphael states that Smith, while still regarding benevolence as "a more commendable virtue," merely places "more stress on other virtuous motives, self-command, the sense of duty" in his second work. Raphael also gives a lucid summary of major critics' views regarding the discrepancy in Smith's two works. See D. D. Raphael, *Adam Smith*, 69-80, 86-101. See also D. D.

Raphael and A. L. Macfie, Introduction, in Smith, *Theory* 20-22. A. L. Macfie, along the same line, argues that both works present a consistent point of view. But Macfie ignores Smith's emphasis on sympathy as a virtue in his first work and concludes that Smith tries to show that sympathy is a form of self-love. Macfie's argument, though eloquent, is thus not convincing in this aspect. See A. L. Macfie, "Adam Smith's *Moral Sentiments* as Foundation for His *Wealth of Nations*," *Oxford Economic Papers* 11 (October, 1959): 209-28. For a recent criticism and discussion of Adam Smith's theory of "self-interest," see Kenneth Lux, *Adam Smith's Mistake: How a Moral Philosopher Invented Economics and Ended Morality* (Boston: Shambhala, 1990), particularly 80-93.

12. Smith, *Wealth* 423.

13. See Wilson Carey McWilliams, *The Idea of Fraternity in America* (Berkeley: U of California P, 1973) 387.

14. Howells first encountered Gronlund's work in 1888. He called it a prophecy of "the total change of our polity, and the reconstruction of our society" based on a new principle in the future. And later he observed that Bellamy's *Looking Backward*, a book that he highly recommended, was constructed almost exactly upon the lines of . . . [*The*] *Cooperative Commonwealth*." See Everett Carter, Introduction, in Howells xv-xvi.

15. Laurence Gronlund, *The Cooperative Commonwealth* (1884; Cambridge, MA: Belknap 1965) 220.

16. Gronlund 220.

17. Gronlund 35.

18. Gronlund 221.

19. Gronlund 222.

20. Gronlund 223.

21. Gronlund 220.

22. Gronlund 223.

23. Gronlund considered his book as one leading "indirectly, and probably unconsciously," to Bellamy's *Looking Backward*, though Bellamy denied any of Gronlund's direct influence on his work. See Albert Fried, *Socialism in America* (New York: Doubleday, 1970) 260, 266.

24. Edward Bellamy, *Looking Backward* (Boston: Houghton, 1966) 6-7.

25. Bellamy 7.

26. Bellamy 92-93.

27. Edward Bellamy, "Looking Forward," in Fried 320-21.

28. See, for example, Van Wyck Brooks, *Howells: His Life and World* (New York: Dutton, 1959) 177-78. Brooks lists five major sources that exerted influence on Howells's socialist views in the 1880s: (1) his father's utopian aspirations; (2) Tolstoy; (3) Zola; (4) Gronlund; and (5) Bellamy. Other critics, such as Everett Carter

and Kenneth S. Lynn, more or less agree on this point, though with slight differences. Carter, for example, emphasizes the Haymarket tragedy. See Carter, Introduction, in Howells xiv-xvii. Also see Kenneth S. Lynn, *William Dean Howells: An American Life* (New York: Jovanovich, 1971) 290-96.

29. William Dean Howells, "Editor's Study," *Harper's Monthly*, LXXVI (April 1888): 802, qtd. in Carter, Introduction, in Howells xv.

30. William Dean Howells, *The Rise of Silas Lapham* (1885; Bloomington: Indiana UP, 1971) 194.

31. Paul Avrich, *The Haymarket Tragedy* (NJ: Princeton UP, 1984) 215-19.

32. Henry David, *History of the Haymarket Affair* (Farrar, 1936) 528, qtd. in Avrich 215.

33. Avrich 215.

34. *The Knights of Labor*, May 8, 1886, qtd. in Avrich 220.

35. Avrich 280.

36. See Avrich 280, 282.

37. William Dean Howells to Francis Fisher Browne, November 4, 1887, *Chicago Tribune*, November 8, 1887, qtd. in Avrich 301.

38. Clara and Rudolf Kirk, "William Dean Howells, George William Curtis, and the Haymarket Affair," *American Literature* 40 (1969): 490-91, qtd. in Avrich 301-02.

39. Mildred Howells, ed., *Life in Letters of William Dean Howells* (1928; New York: Russell, 1968) 1: 393.

40. Lynn 290.

41. Lynn 291.

42. Lynn 291.

43. William Dean Howells to Thomas S. Perry, April 14, 1888, in Howells, *Life in Letters* 398-99.

44. Edwin H. Cady, *The Realist at War* (Syracuse: Syracuse UP, 1956) 72-73.

45. H. M. Alden to William Dean Howells, November 13, 1888, qtd. in Carter, Introduction, in *Howells* xv. See also Carter, *Howells and the Age of Realism* (Philadelphia: Lippincott, 1954) 185-86.

46. William Dean Howells to Annie Howells, November 18, 1887, in Howells, *Life in Letters* 1: 404.

47. Anarchism, a political movement, was economically motivated. In America, anarchists were generally recognized as labor agitators, calling the working class to be engaged in a direct confrontation with capital for political and economical improvements. After the Haymarket incident, the anarchists were labeled as "robbers" and "thieves." Avrich 55-67, 215-20.

48. Howells, *Life in Letters* 1: 404.

49. The novel is generally seen to bear the mark of Tolstoyanism. Lynn, however,

argues that it is "actually a rebuttal of Tolstoy" because the major character pays an intolerable price for his Tolstoyan belief and practice. See Lynn 293.

50. William Dean Howells, *Annie Kilburn* (New York: Harper, 1889) 65.

51. Howells, *Kilburn* 169.

52. Howells, *Kilburn* 324.

53. Howells, *Kilburn* 230-33.

54. Howells, *Kilburn* 325.

55. Carter, *Howells* 194.

56. Cady 99.

57. Amy Kaplan points out that the "L" has "a double-edged effect": it expands the Marches' perspective, and it dislocates what they see by covering up the misery of the city. See Amy Kaplan, "'The Knowledge of the Line': Realism and the City in Howells' *A Hazard of New Fortunes*," *PMLA* 101 (1986): 72-73.

58. William Sumner Jenkins, *Pro-Slavery Thought in the Old South* (Chapel Hill: U of North Caroline P, 1935) 298

59. Howell Cobb, *A Scriptural Examination of the Institution of Slavery in the United States* ([Perry] (sic), Georgia, 1856) 214, qtd. in Jenkins 298. The same view was reiterated in many pro-slavery writings and was examined in scholarly works, such as Ulrich Bonnell Phillips's influential book, *American Negro Slavery* (New York: Appleton, 1928), Robert William Fogel and Stanley L. Engerman's *Time On the Cross* (Boston: Little, 1974), and Jenkins's work.

60. James Henley Thornwell, D. D., *Hear the South! The State of the Country: An Article Republished from the* Southern Presbyterian Review (Columbia, 1861) 46, qtd. in Jenkins 110.

61. George Fitzhugh, *Sociology for the South, or the Failure of Free Society* (Richmond, 1854) 67-68, qtd. in Jenkins 298.

62. The Marches make the acquaintance of Margaret Vance at the reception. On their way home, they comment on the combination of "intellectual fashionableness and worldly innocence" in Margaret. March says, "For such an exquisite creature as Miss Vance . . . we couldn't pay too much" (250). While March's statement points out the rarity of such a saint-like creature, it magnifies Margaret's selflessness in her disseminating sympathy to "the destitute." However, a few pages later, Howells comments, not without irony, that Margaret is "the kind of girl that might have fancies for artists and poets, but might end by marrying a prosperous broker and leavening a vast lump of moneyed and fashionable life, with her culture, generosity, and good-will" (254). Such a tragic ending, Howells suggests, is caused by social pressure because Margaret, as a girl, is after all only "a by-law," subject to the control of law, the general expectation of the society and even her aunt Mrs. Horn (252-54).

63. The protagonist March is generally identified with Howells. In his discussion of March's change of view regarding the relation between esthetics and morality,

Kermit Vanderbilt parallels the change with that of Howells and shows a close resemblance between the two. See Kermit Vanderbilt, *The Achievement of William Dean Howells: A Reinterpretation* (Princeton: Princeton UP, 1986) 159-68.

64. Howells's view of "complicity" was formulated after the Haymarket event, an incident that proved to Howells that complicity was the truth of modern human affairs. For a discussion of March's understanding of complicity, see Carter, *Howells* 206, or Cady 110-11.

65. The ending of the novel has often been discussed and debated. Vanderbilt, for example, thinks that the "ultimate meaning" of the novel is clouded by the inconclusiveness and vagueness of its ending, which reveal a basic disharmony in Howells's esthetic of realism, that is, Howells's own uncertainty about his conclusions in regard to "realism" and social reform. Bennett disputes Vanderbilt's point by arguing that the ending is "open" rather than "inconclusive." The openness of the ending is neither a sign of failure to find solutions to the economic problems nor that of evasiveness resulting from the desire to avoid didacticism. It is rather a deliberate refusal and an appropriate conclusion to the novel. See Vanderbilt 179-91, and Bennett, *Realism* 36, 38.

66. On this point, I strongly disagree with Bennett who regards it as an "irony" that "Conrad's death neither changes Dryfoos nor brings him greater understanding." See Bennett, *Howells* 192. In Dryfoos's willingness to transfer the ownership of the magazine and his penitence toward Conrad and Lindau, we see a stricken or awakened conscience caused by Conrad's death.

67. William Dean Howells, *Literature and Life* (New York: Kennikat, 1968) 31-33.

68. Howells, *Literature* 25.

69. Howells, *Literature* 9.

70. William Dean Howells, "Editor's Study," *Harper's* 72 (May, 1886) 973, qtd. in Wai-Chee Dimock, "Economy of Pain," *New Essays on The Rise of Silas Lapham*, ed. Donald Pease (Cambridge: Cambridge UP, 1991) 75.

71. Smith, *Theory* 38-39.

72. Howells, *Life in Letters* 1: 404.

73. Howells's ambivalence is traceable in his argument, his attitude toward the competitive mode, and his view of the marketplace in "The Man of Letters as A Man of Business": while contending that literature as business is the "opprobrium of literature," he teaches young writers to be good businessmen; while labeling the writer as "a working man," he refuses to identify the writer with a producer; while defending the sublimity of literature, he complains that works of truly high quality are rarely appreciated and thus not popular. See Howells, *Literature* 1-35.

74. Kenneth S. Lynn, *Visions of America* (Westport, CT: Greenwood, 1973) 63.

75. See Vanderbilt 142, and Lynn 63.

76. Howells, *Life in Letters* 2: 1.

77. Howells, *Life in Letters* 1: 417.

Chapter III: Economy of Attention

1. Henry Blake Fuller, *With the Procession* (Harper, 1895; Chicago: U of Chicago, 1965) 105, 106. The novel is hereafter referred to by *WP* and page number in the text.

2. *Oxford English Dictionary* (Oxford: Clarendon, 2nd ed., 1989).

3. Everett Carter points out that Fuller's works underlined Herbert Spencer's doctrine of "the economy of attention." But Carter gives no further elaboration of this point. See Everett Carter, *Howells and the Age of Realism* (Lippincott, 1954) 255. Herbert Spencer discusses this issue of attention with a focus on linguistic phenomena in a number of essays, among which "The Philosophy of Style" gives this subject a most thorough treatment. Spencer argues that the great force of Saxon English "first claims our attention," and he illustrates that "economy" is "the secret" of this effect by demonstrating the right choice of words, arrangement of clauses, use of figurative speech, and the rhythmical sequence of syllables. See Herbert Spencer, "The Philosophy of Style," *Essays: Moral, Political and Aesthetic* (New York: Appleton, 1881) 9-47.

4. Thorstein Veblen, *The Theory of the Leisure Class* (1899; New York: NAL, 1953) 26.

5. Veblen 32.

6. Veblen 70.

7. See Veblen, particularly 33-79.

8. Thorstein Veblen, "The Economic Theory of Woman's Dress," *Popular Science Monthly* 46 (1895): 198-205.

9. See Wiebe 41.

10. Hugh Dalziel Duncan, *Culture and Democracy* (Totowa, NJ: Bedminster, 1965) 95.

11. Henry Blake Fuller, "The Upward Movement in Chicago," *Atlantic Monthly* 80 (1897): 545.

12. Morris, *Dictionary of Chicago*, 29, qtd. in Daniel Bluestone, *Constructing Chicago* (New Haven: Yale UP, 1991) 112.

13. Harvey Warren Zorbaugh, *The Gold Coast and the Slum* (1929; Chicago: U of Chicago P, 1976) 2.

14. See Carl S. Smith, *Chicago and the American Literary Imagination: 1880-1920* (Chicago: U of Chicago P, 1984) 140-42. For relevant discussions, see also William Dean Howells, *Letters of an Altrurian Traveller:1893-1894* (Gainesville, Florida: Scholar's Facsimiles and Reprints, 1961) 20-34; Henry Adams, *The Education of Henry Adams* (1918; Boston: Houghton, 1961) 339-41; and Neil Harris, *Cultural Excursions* (Chicago: U of Chicago P, 1990) 111-31.

15. David Lowe, *Lost Chicago* (Boston: Houghton, 1975) 152.

16. Robert Herrick, "Myself" (Robert Herrick Papers, Box 3, Folder 10, University of

Chicago Archives) 48-49, qtd. in Smith 147.

17. Herrick 48-49, qtd. in Smith 147.

18. Theodore Dreiser, *A Book about Myself* (New York: Boni and Liveright, 1922) 246, 247.

19. Smith 143.

20. Neil Harris discusses the dualism—the exterior monumentalism and the interior objective and active world—in his work *Cultural Excursions* (Chicago: U of Chicago P, 1990), particularly 119-21. See also Siegfried Giedion, *Mechanization Takes Command* (New York: Oxford UP, 1948) 395.

21. Edgar Kaufmann and Ben Raeburn, eds., *Frank Lloyd Wright: Writings and Buildings* (1960; Cleveland, Ohio: World Publishing, 1970) 29-30.

22. Louis Sullivan, *The Autobiography of an Idea* (1924; New York: Dover, 1956) 324, 325.

23. See, for example, "World's Fair Architecture," *The Morning News Record* 14 Sept. 1892: 4; 16 Sept. 1892: 4; 20 Sept. 1892: 4; "Minor Buildings at the Fair," *The Chicago Record* 2 June 1893: 4; 5 June 1893: 4. For a more detailed list of these articles, see Kenneth Scambray, *A Varied Harvest: The Life and Works of Henry Blake Fuller* (Pittsburgh: U of Pittsburgh P, 1987) 180-81.

24. Fuller, "World's Fair Architecture" 14 Sept. 1892: 4.

25. Fuller, "World's Fair Architecture" 4.

26. Fuller, "World's Fair Architecture" 4.

27. Fuller, "The Upward Movement in Chicago" 534.

28. Fuller, "The Upward Movement in Chicago" 535-47.

29. Fuller, "The Upward Movement in Chicago" 547.

30. See Christopher Lasch, *The Culture of Narcissism* (New York: Norton, 1979) 52-70. Lasch makes a historical examination of the evolution of America's attitude toward success, from its origin in the Puritan work ethic to its modern manifestation in the entrepreneur.

31. Lasch 60.

32. John G. Cawelti, *Apostles of the Self-Made Man* (Chicago: U of Chicago P, 1965) 183. Cawelti's review of the self-help books shows a gradual moral transition toward an emphasis on personal magnetism in the nineteenth century.

33. Cawelti 183. Cawelti further points out that the "New Thought" movement, influenced by the popular pseudosciences of phrenology, animal magnetism, spiritualism, and mesmerism, reinforced the trend for personal magnetism and "symbolized the final breakdown of the old ideal of self-improvement." See Cawelti 183.

34. George Horace Lorimer, *Letters from a Self-Made Merchant to His Son* (Boston: Small, 1903) 35-40, 87-89, and 127-28.

35. John Walker Harrington, "Ottenhausen's Coup," *McClure's Magazine* 10 (1897-98): 481.

36. Andrew Carnegie, "Wealth," *North American Review* 148 (1889): 653-64. The article was later renamed as "The Gospel of Wealth."

37. Carnegie seemed to repudiate material showiness in his suggestion for the wealthy to lead "a modest, unostentatious living, shunning display or extravagance." Carnegie admonished that the man of wealth was "the mere trustee," administering for his poorer brethren, and the wealth accumulated should be subsequently returned back to society. But Carnegie's proposal for the disposal of accumulated wealth was fundamentally a call for seeking social attention. Giving philanthropic donations easily brought the wealthy into more public attention: with an ever enduring effect on a possibly wide range of beneficiaries, it brought attention to the person of good will. The distribution of immense charities, another form of sumptuous extravagance, demonstrated what Veblen called the traces of "invidious comparison" and signaled the competition for superior pecuniary strength. Carnegie's theory was supported by his own passionate practice in establishing the Andrew Carnegie Relief Fund, aiding American colleges, and constructing libraries and numerous other solid three-dimensional monuments to his wealth and success. See Andrew Carnegie, *Autobiography of Andrew Carnegie* (1920; Boston: Northeastern UP, 1986) 245-66. Carnegie's autobiography is evenly proportioned, i.e., the first third is about his railroad experience; the second third about the period of acquisition; and the last third about the period of distribution, devoted to the philanthropic activities. The proportion of the third part indicates that Carnegie's success in seeking attention through donation shares an equal significance as the other two periods.

38. Yoshinobu Hakutani, ed. *Selected Magazine Articles of Theodore Dreiser* (New York: Associated UP, 1985) 162-63.

39. Hakutani 163.

40. Zorbaugh 80.

41. John Pilkington, Jr., *Henry Blake Fuller* (New York: Twayne, 1970) 88. Pilkington considers the Clifton as a good but failed symbol since the symbol becomes subordinate to the melodramatic events in the Brainard family and George Ogden's marriage in the last third and the book contains "a horde of minor characters." See Pilkington 96.

42. Bernard R. Bowron, Jr., *Henry B. Fuller of Chicago* (Westport, CT: Greenwood, 1974) 143. Bowron notes that Fuller, when working on *The Cliff-Dwellers*, must have had in mind "the Home Insurance Building, completed in 1885 and regarded by most historians of architecture as the world's first true skyscraper." Bowron further notes that Fuller was "probably the first American novelist acutely conscious of the possibilities of the new American city as material for literary art." See Bowron 129n.

43. Robert C. Bray, *Rediscoveries: Literature and Place in Illinois* (Urbana: U of Illinois P, 1982) 100-01.

44. Bray 98.

45. Bray 106.

46. Henry Blake Fuller, *The Cliff-Dwellers* (Harper, 1893; Ridgewood, NJ: Gregg, 1968) 4. The novel is hereafter referred to by *CD* and page number in the text.

47. Henry Blake Fuller, "The Shortcomings of Our Architects," *The Saturday Evening Post* 6 Oct. 1900: 12.

48. Veblen, *The Theory of the Leisure Class* 78.

49. See Veblen, *The Theory of the Leisure Class* 120-21, 126-27.

50. Veblen, *The Theory of the Leisure Class* 54. Veblen's chapter on "conspicuous leisure" details some of the quasi-scholarly or quasi-artistic achievements that serve as an ostentatious evidence of one's leisure and freedom from productive labor.

51. Veblen, *The Theory of the Leisure Class* 47.

52. Mrs. Bates is one of the most deceptive and pretentious women in these two novels. She is so well masked that quite a few critics take her as having "no pretensions." Toby Rita Leff, for instance, states that Sue Bates "regards her background, her elegant home, and her social position with honesty and humor." See Toby Rita Leff, "Technique and Thought in the Work of Henry Blake Fuller," diss., New York U, 1974, 186.

53. These two terms, "pecuniary emulation" and "invidious comparison," borrowed from Veblen, are used in "a technical sense" to describe the phenomenon of rating and grading each other in modern society.

54. Veblen, *The Theory of the Leisure Class* 28-29.

55. Duncan 114.

56. Guy Szuberla's article "Henry Blake Fuller and the 'New Immigrant'" is a focused discussion of Fuller's evolving views and various presentations of the new immigrant in his works at various stages of his literary career. See *American Literature* 53:2 (1981): 246-65.

57. Lasch 59, 60.

58. In *Absentee Ownership and Business Enterprise in Recent Tim*es (1923; New York: Viking, 1964), Veblen explains how the "captain of industry" has gradually evolved and bifurcated into the captain of business and his management team. He also points out that the captain of business exercises "absentee ownership" and demonstrates competence since his ownership of means is shown to be "in excess of what . . . [he] can make use of, personally and without help." See Veblen, *Absentee Ownership* 12-13, 103-08.

59. In his analysis of the novel, Bowron pints out the force of industrialism in shaping business and social life. See Bowron 137. Leff has noticed that the destruction of the Marshalls' garden illustrates the detrimental effect of industrialism. See Leff 215-16.

60. Fuller, "Howells or James?" *Howells: A Century of Criticism*, ed. Kenneth E. Eble (Dallas: Southern Methodist UP, 1962) 34-40.

61. See Fuller, "Howells" 36-39. Fuller's realism clearly deviates from the realism in most of Henry James's novels, as Fuller tends to give a panoramic vista of the social milieu and intense treatment of the contemporary socioeconomic activities, and it also differs from Howells's in its adoption of symbolic forms. Fuller's comment on Chekov some twenty years later draws on the subject again. Fuller views realism not as an impartial recording of facts; rather it has a deliberately designed form and shape to be art, just as the Clifton is used to structure the novel of *The Cliff-Dwellers*. For a relevant discussion, see Leff 169, and Bowron xxii-xxiii.

62. Fuller, "Howells" 39.

63. Fuller, "Howells" 39.

64. Over a decade prior to his writing of these two novels, Fuller had already laid bare his distaste for materialism and against the economy of attention in a long, prosaic poem entitled "*Pensieri Privati*."

 You think me then dissatisfied? and so
 I am, I am. Pray where should discontent
 Grow ranker than just here, 'mongst men intent
 On non-essentials, empty, earth-bound, low.

 See Henry Blake Fuller, Diary for 25 Aug. 1876-24 Feb. 1879, Newberry Library, qtd. in Scambray 48.

65. Fuller, "Howells" 39.

66. Fuller, "Howells" 38.

67. A couple of other examples in *The Cliff-Dwellers* explicate the relation between social realities and realistic novels. Theodore Brower, for example, after discussing Ogden's unhappy marriage with his roommate, picks a book to read. The title of the book, both incidentally and expectedly, is "A Mistaken Marriage." Brower's roommate announces, "It's late" (*CD* 274). This very belatedness underscores the mimetic nature of the realistic novel. The novel "A False Start" is another example. Ogden reads this novel before his marriage with Jessie and leaves it with Bower. After Jessie's death, Ogden returns and discusses life and marriage with Bower, where Ogden sees the book again. He picks up the book and reads the title. He then admits regretfully, "Yes, perhaps it is" (*CD* 317). This "cheap novel" surely has given a right prediction, and it offers a new direction as Ogden, after reading the book in the following two nights, makes up his mind and goes to the West Side to meet with Abbie Brainard.

68. Henry Blake Fuller, "My Early Books," Newberry Library, qtd. in Bowron 127-28.

69. Pilkington 90. Many marriages mentioned in these two novels clearly prove Veblen's point that a wife's extravagance is the visible sign of her husband's pecuniary strength. Without such a material support, the extravagance of the wife could only lead to disasters, as shown in Ogden's marriage with Jessie. For a relevant discussion on this, see Pilkington 90, and Bowron 134-35. Fuller's two novels, to some extent, may be seen as an encyclopedia of marriages. In *The Cliff-Dwellers*, for example, over a dozen married couples are depicted, and their marriages are discussed. While showing that most of these marriages appear happy, Fuller satiri-

cally exposes the pecuniary factor as corrosive, debasing foundation. For a relevant discussion, see Scambray 87-88.

70. Not interested in a superficial glamorous life-style, Brower gives attention to the poor and appeals to curb social inequality. To this extent, Brower is what Bray considers the ethical center in the novel. And Bray defines Brower as "a man firmly grounded in the social reality of life." See Bray 104-05.

71. Bowron has overlooked the formal function of these marriages as he interprets the endings of these novels as a lapse into the "conventional marriage-choice motif." See Bowron 136.

72. Fuller, "My Early Books," qtd. in Bowron 128.

Bibliography

I. Primary Sources

Fuller, Henry Blake. *Cliff-Dwellers*. 1893. Ridgewood, NJ: Gregg, 1968.

———. "Howells or James?" *Howells: A Century of Criticism*. Ed. Kenneth E. Eble. Dallas: Southern Methodist UP, 1962. 34-40.

———. "The Upward Movement in Chicago." *Atlantic Monthly* 80 (1897): 545.

———. *With the Procession*. 1895. Chicago: U of Chicago P, 1965.

Howells, Mildred, ed. *Life in The Letters of William Dean Howells*. 1928. New York: Russell, 1968. 2 vols.

Howells, William Dean. *A Hazard of New Fortunes*. 1890. Bloomington: Indiana UP, 1976.

———. *Annie Kilburn*. New York: Harper, 1889.

———. *Criticism and Fiction*. Eds. Clara M. Kirk and Rudolf Kirk. New York: New York UP, 1959.

———. "The Man of Letters as a Man of Business." *Literature and Life*. Ed. William Dean Howells. New York: Kennikat, 1968. 1-35.

———. *The Rise of Silas Lapham*. 1885. Bloomington: Indiana UP, 1971.

Twain, Mark. "A New Crime." *The Writings of Mark Twain*. Vol. 19. New York: Harper, 1906. 244-50.

Twain, Mark and Charles Dudley Warner. *The Gilded Age*. Hartford: American, 1873.

———. *The Gilded Age*. London: Routledge, 1874. 3 vols.

II. Secondary Sources

A. On The Cultural Context:

Bronner, Simon J., ed. *Consuming Visions*. New York: Norton, 1989.

Cawelti, John. *Apostles of the Self-Made Man*. Chicago: U of Chicago P, 1965.

Chandler, Alfred. *The Essential Chandler*. Boston: Harvard Business

School P, 1988.
———. *The Visible Hand.* Cambridge, MA: Belknap, 1977.
Cochran, Thomas C., and William Miller. *The Age of Enterprise: A Social History of Industrial America.* New York: Harper, 1961.
Curti, Merle. *The Growth of American Thought.* New York: Harper, 1943.
———. *A History of American Civilization.* 1953. New York: Books for Libraries, 1969.
Fox, Richard W., and T. J. Lears, eds. *The Culture of Consumption: Critical Essays in American History 1880-1980.* New York: Pantheon, 1983.
Giedion, Siegfried. *Mechanization Takes Command.* New York: Oxford UP, 1948.
Hacker, Louis M. *American Capitalism: Its Promise and Accomplishment.* Princeton, NJ: Van Nostrand, 1957.
———. *The Course of American Economic Growth and Development.* New York: Wiley, 1970.
Hofstadter, Richard. *Social Darwinism in American Thought.* Rev. ed. New York: Braziller, 1959.
Josephson, Matthew. *The Robber Barons.* 1934; New York: Harcourt, 1962.
Kirkland, Edward Chase. *Dream and Thought in the Business Community, 1860-1900.* Ithaca: Cornell UP, 1956.
———. *Industry Comes of Age: Business, Labor, and Public Policy, 1860-1897.* Chicago: Quadrangle, 1961.
Rischin, Moses, ed. *The American Gospel of Success.* Chicago: Quadrangle, 1965.
Scharnhorst, Gary. *The Lost Life of Horatio Alger, Jr.* Bloomington, Indiana UP, 1985.
Sorokin, Pitirim. *Social and Cultural Mobility.* Illinois: Free, 1959.
Tebbel, John. *From Rags to Riches.* New York: Macmillan, 1963.
Trachtenberg, Alan. *The Incorporation of America: Culture and Society in the Gilded Age.* New York: Hill, 1982.
Wyllie, Irvin G. *The Self-Made Man in America: The Myth of Rags to Riches.* New Brunswick: Rutgers UP, 1954.

B. General Literary Criticism:

Banta, Martha. *Failure and Success in America: A Literary Debate.* Princeton: Princeton UP, 1979.

Bell, Michael Davitt. *The Problem of American Realism.* Chicago: U of Chicago P, 1993.

Bercovitch, Sacvan. *The American Jeremiad. Madison*: U of Wisconsin P, 1978.

———, ed. *Reconstructing American Literary History.* Cambridge, MA: Harvard UP, 1986.

Berthoff, Warner. *The Ferment of Realism.* New York: Free, 1965.

Bewley, Marius. *The Eccentric Design: Form in the Classic American Novel.* New York: Columbia UP, 1963.

Borus, Daniel H. *Writing Realism: Howells, James, and Norris in the Mass Market.* Chapel Hill: U of North Carolina P, 1989.

Cady, Edwin H. *The Light of Common Day.* Bloomington: Indiana UP, 1971.

Dietrichson, Jan W. *The Image of Money.* New York: Humanities, 1969.

Dimock, Wai-Chee. "Degrading Exchange: Edith Wharton's House of Mirth." *PMLA* 100 (1985): 783-92.

Eagleton, Terry. *Criticism and Ideology.* London: Verso, 1976.

———. "Text, Ideology, Realism." *Literature and Society.* Ed. Edward Said. Baltimore: Johns Hopkins UP, 1980. 149-73.

Elliott, Emory, ed. *Columbia Literary History of the United States.* New York: Columbia UP, 1988.

Fisher, Philip. *Hard Facts.* New York: Oxford UP, 1985.

Flory, Claude Reherd. *Economic Criticism in American Fiction 1792 to 1900.* Philadelphia: n.p., 1936.

Fried, Lewis F. *Makers of the City.* Amherst: U of Massachusetts P, 1990.

Gilmore, Michael. *American Romanticism and the Marketplace.* Chicago: U of Chicago P, 1985.

Godden, Richard. *Fictions of Capital: The American Novel from James to Mailer.* Cambridge: Cambridge UP, 1990.

Goux, Jean-Joseph. *Symbolic Economies: After Marx and Freud.* Ithaca, NY: Cornell UP, 1990.

Horwitz, Howard. *By the Law of Nature: Form and Value in Nineteenth-Century America.* NY: Oxford UP, 1991.

Howard, June. *Form and History in American Literary Naturalism.* Chapel Hill: U of North Carolina P, 1985.

Jameson, Fredric. *Marxism and Form*. Princeton: Princeton UP, 1971.

———. *The Political Unconscious*. Ithaca: Cornell UP, 1981.

Kaplan, Amy. *Social Construction of American Realism*. Chicago: U of Chicago P, 1988.

Kolb, Harold H., Jr. *The Illusion of Life*. Charlottesville: UP of Virginia, 1969.

Lukacs, Georg. *The Theory of Novel*. Trans. Anna Rostock. 1920. Cambridge, MA: MIT P, 1978.

Macherey, Pierre. *A Theory of Literary Production*. French ed. Trans. Geoffrey Wall. London: Routledge, 1978.

Martin, Jay. *Harvests of Change: American Literature 1865-1914*. Englewood Cliffs, NJ: Prentice, 1967.

Michaels, Walter Benn. *The Gold Standard and the Logic of Naturalism*. Berkeley: U of California P, 1987.

Miller, D. A. *Narrative and Its Discontents*. Princeton, NJ: Princeton UP, 1981.

Papashvily, Helen Waite. *All the Happy Endings*. New York: Kennikat P, 1956.

Parrington, V. L. *The Beginnings of Critical Realism in America: 1860-1920*. New York: Harcourt, 1930.

Poirier, Richard. *A World Elsewhere*. New York: Oxford UP, 1966.

Porter, Carolyn. *Seeing and Being*. Conn.: Wesleyan UP, 1981.

Shell, Marc. *Money, Language and Thought*. Berkeley: U of California P, 1982.

———. *The Economy of Literature*. Baltimore: Johns Hopkins UP, 1978.

Shulman, Robert. *Social Criticism and Nineteenth-Century American Fiction*. Columbia: U of Missouri P, 1987.

Simmel, Georg. *The Philosophy of Money*. Boston: Routledge, 1978.

Sundquist, Eric, ed. *American Realism: New Essays*. Baltimore: Johns Hopkins UP, 1982.

Taylor, Walter F. *The Economic Novel in America*. Chapel Hill: U of North Carolina P, 1942.

Tucker, Robert. *The Marx-Engels Reader*. New York: Norton, 1972.

Vernon, John. *Money and Fiction*. Ithaca: Cornell UP, 1984.

Weber, Max. *The Protestant Ethic and the Spirit of Capitalism*. New York: Scribner, 1958.

C. On Mark Twain and *The Gilded Age*:

Andrews, Kenneth R. *Nook Farm*. Cambridge, MA: Harvard UP, 1950.

Bassett, John E. "The Gilded Age: Performance, Power, and Authority." *Studies in the Novel* 17 (1985): 395-405.

Bellamy, Gladys Carmen. *Mark Twain as a Literary Artist*. Norman: U of Oklahoma P, 1950.

Biggs, John, Jr. *The Guilty Mind: Psychiatry and the Law of Homicide*. Baltimore: Johns Hopkins UP, 1955.

Brooks, Van Wyck. *The Ordeal of Mark Twain*. Rev. ed. New York: Dutton, 1933.

Budd, Louis. *Mark Twain: Social Philosopher*. Bloomington: Indiana UP, 1962.

Cardwell, Guy. *The Man Who Was Mark Twain*. New Haven: Yale UP, 1991.

Carr, William Wilkins. *The Suggestion of Insanity and the Trial of the Collateral Issue*. Philadelphia: Johnson, 1890.

Dain, Normain. *Concepts of Insanity in the United States, 1789-1865*. New Brunswick, NJ: Rutgers UP, 1964.

DeVoto, Bernard Augustine. *Mark Twain's America*. Boston: Little, 1932.

Fisher, Philip. "Mark Twain." *Elliott* 627-44.

Foner, Philip. *Mark Twain: Social Critic*. 2nd ed. New York: International, 1972.

French, Bryant Morey. *Mark Twain and The Gilded Age*. Dallas: Southern Methodist UP, 1965.

Gillman, Susan. *Dark Twins*. Chicago: U of Chicago P, 1989.

Goldstein, Abraham S. *The Insanity Defense*. New Haven: Yale UP, 1967.

Harris, Susan. "Mark Twain's Bad Women." *Studies in American Fiction* 13 (1985): 157-68.

Hughes, John Starrett. *In the Law's Darkness: Isaac Ray and the Medical Jurisprudence of Insanity in Nineteenth-Century America*. New York: Oceana, 1986.

Kaplan, Justin. *Mr. Clemens and Mark Twain*. New York: Simon, 1966.

Lenz, William E. *Fast Talk and Flush Times: The Confidence Man as a Literary Convention*. Columbia: U of Missouri P, 1985.

Maeder, Thomas. *Crime and Madness: The Origins and the Evolution of the Insanity Defense*. New York: Harper, 1985.

Nicolson, David. "The Measure of Individual and Social Responsibility in Criminal Cases." *British Journal of Psychiatry* 24 (1878): 1+.

O'Brien, Jerry. "'Everybody Chases Butterflies': The Theme of False Hope in The Gilded Age." *Journal of American Culture* 6: 69-75.

Rosenberg, Charles E. *The Trial of the Assassin Guiteau.* Chicago: U of Chicago P, 1968.

Sax, Richard. "Living in the Realm of Possibility: Beriah Sellers in The Gilded Age." *Mark Twain Journal* 21 (1983): 38-41.

Schmitz, Neil. "Mark Twain, Henry James, and Jacksonian Dreaming." *Criticism* 27 (1985): 155-73.

Sewell, David R. *Mark Twain's Languages.* Berkeley: U of California P, 1987.

Smith, Henry Nash. *Mark Twain's Fable of Progress.* New Brunswick, NJ: Rutgers UP, 1964.

Thoreson, Trygve. "Mark Twain's Unsentimental Heroine." *The South Carolina Review* 14 (1982): 22-32.

D. On William Dean Howells and *A Hazard of New Fortunes*:

Aaron, Daniel. *The Unwritten War.* New York: Knopf, 1973.

Arms, George. "Howells's New York Novel: Comedy and Belief." *Critics on William Dean Howells.* Ed. Paul A. Escholz. Coral Gables: U of Miami P, 1975. 102-11.

Avrich, Paul. *The Haymarket Tragedy.* Princeton, NJ: Princeton UP, 1984.

Bassett, John E. "'A Heart of Ideality in My Realism': Howells's Early Criticism." *Papers on Language and Literature* 25 (1989): 67-82.

Bellamy, Edward. *Looking Backward.* 1888. Boston: Houghton, 1966.

———. "Looking Forward." *The Nationalist* 1 (1889). Rpt. in *Socialism in America.* By Albert Fried. New York: Doubleday, 1970. 320-23.

Bennett, George N. *The Realism of William Dean Howells: 1889-1920.* Nashville, TN: Vanderbilt UP, 1973.

———. *William Dean Howells: The Development of a Novelist.* Norman: U of Oklahoma P, 1959.

Brooks, Van Wyck. *Howells: His Life and World.* New York: Dutton, 1959.

Cady, Edwin H. *The Realist at War.* Syracuse, NY: Syracuse UP 1958.

Cady, Edwin H., and Norma W. Cady, eds. *Critical Essays on William*

Dean Howells, 1866-1920. Boston: Hall, 1983.

Carter, Everett. *Howells and the Age of Realism*. Philadelphia: Dippincott, 1950.

———. Introduction. *Howells, A Hazard of New Fortunes*. xi-ixxx.

———. "The Haymarket Affair in Literature." *The American Quarterly* 2 (1950): 270-78.

Crowley, John W. "Howells in the Eighties: A Review of Criticism, Part II." *ESQ* 33 (1987): 45-65.

Dimock, Wai-Chee. "The Economy of Pain: The Case of Howells." *Raritan* 9 (1990): 99-119. Rpt. as "The Economy of Pain: Capitalism, Humanitarianism, and the Realistic Novel." *New Essays on the Rise of Silas Lapham*. Ed. Donald Pease. Cambridge: Cambridge UP, 1991. 67-90.

Dooley, Patrick K. "Moral Purpose in Howells' Realism." *American Studies* 25 (1984): 75-77.

Eble, Kenneth E., ed. *Howells: A Century of Criticism*. Dallas: Southern Methodist UP, 1962.

———. *William Dean Howells*. 2nd ed. Boston: Twayne, 1982.

Garlin, Sender. *William Dean Howells and the Haymarket Era*. New York: The American Institute for Marxist Studies, 1979.

Gronlund, Laurence. *The Cooperative Commonwealth*. 1884. Cambridge, MA: Belknap, 1965.

Hough, Robert L. *The Quiet Rebel*. 1959. N.p.: Atchon, 1968.

Howells, Mildred, ed. *Life and Letters of William Dean Howells*. 2 vols. New York: Russell, 1968.

Kaplan, Amy. "'The Knowledge of the Line: Realism and the City in Howells' A Hazard of New Fortunes." *PMLA* 101 (1986): 72-73.

Lynn, Kenneth S. *Visions of America*. Westport, CT: Greenwood, 1973.

———. *William Dean Howells: An American Life*. New York: Harcourt, 1971.

McWilliams, Carey. *The Idea of Fraternity in America*. Berkeley: U of California P, 1973.

Maffi, Mario. "Architecture in the City, Architecture in the Novel." *Studies in the Literary Imagination* 16 (1983): 35-43.

Scheler, Max. *The Nature of Sympathy*. 1954. London: Routledge, 1970.

Shulman, Robert. *Social Criticism and Nineteenth Century American Fic-*

tions. Columbia: U of Missouri P, 1987.
Smith, Adam. *Lectures on Rhetoric and Belles Lettres*. Ed. J. C. Bryce. Oxford: Clarendon, 1983.
———. *Theory of Moral Sentiments*. 1759. Oxford: Clarendon, 1976.
———. *The Wealth of Nations*. 1776. New York: The Modern Library, 1965.
Spangler, George M. "The Idea of Degeneration in American Fiction 1880-1940." *English Studies* 70 (1989): 407-35.
Spindler, Michael. *American Literature and Social Change: William Dean Howells to Arthur Miller*. Bloomington: Indiana UP, 1983.
Vanderbilt, Kermit. *The Achievement of William Dean Howells: A Reinterpretation*. Princeton, NJ: Princeton UP, 1968.

E. On Henry Blake Fuller, *Cliff-Dwellers* and *With the Procession*:

Blueston, Daniel. *Constructing Chicago*. New Haven: Yale UP, 1991.
Bowron, Bernard R. Jr. *Henry B. Fuller of Chicago*. Westport, CT: Greenwood, 1974.
Bray, Robert C. *Rediscoveries: Literature and Place in Illinois*. Urbana: U of Illinois P, 1982.
Carnegie, Andrew. *Autobiography of Andrew Carnegie*. 1920. Boston: Northeastern UP, 1986.
———. "Wealth." *North American Review* 148 (1889): 653-64.
Duffey, Bernard I. *The Chicago Renaissance in American Letters*. East Lancing, MI: Michigan State UP, 1954.
Duncan, Hugh Dalziel. *Culture and Democracy*. Totowa, NJ: Bedminster, 1965.
———. *The Rise of Chicago as a Literary Center from 1865 to 1920*. NJ: Bedminster, 1964.
Grifflin, Constance. *Henry Blake Fuller: A Critical Biography*. Philadelphia: U of Pennsylvania P, 1939.
Hakutani, Yoshinobu, ed. *Selected Magazine Articles of Theodore Dreiser*. New York: Associated UP, 1985.
Harris, Mark. Introduction. Fuller, *With the Procession* v-xiv.
Lasch, Christopher. *The Culture of Narcissism*. New York: Norton, 1979.
Leff, Toby Rita. "Technique and Thought in the Work of Henry Blake Fuller." Diss. New York U, 1974.
Lorimer, George Horace. *Letters from a Self-Made Merchant to His Son*.

Boston: Small, 1903.

Morton, Sue. "The Fiction of Henry B. Fuller." Diss. U of Wisconsin-Madison, 1978.

Pearce, Richard. "Chicago in the Fiction of the 1890's as Illustrated in the Novels of Henry Blake Fuller and Robert Herrick." Diss. Columbia U, 1963.

Pilkington, John, Jr. *Henry Blake Fuller*. New York: Twayne, 1970.

Scambray, Kenneth. *A Varied Harvest: The Life and Works of Henry Blake Fuller*. Pittsburgh: U of Pittsburgh P, 1987.

———. "The Romance in Decline: Realism in Henry Blake Fuller's Cliff-Dwellers." *North Dakota Quarterly* 46 (1978): 19-28.

Silet, Charles L. P. *Henry Blake Fuller and Hamlin Garland: A Reference Guide*. Boston: Hall, 1977.

Smith, Carl S. *Chicago and the American Literary Imagination 1880-1920*. Chicago: U of Chicago, 1984.

Szuberla, Guy. "Henry Blake Fuller and the 'New Immigrant.'" *American Literature* 53 (1981): 246-65.

———. "Making the Sublime Mechanical: Henry Blake Fuller's Chicago." *American Studies* 14 (1973): 83-93.

Veblen, Thorstein. "The Economic Theory of Woman's Dress." *Popular Science Monthly* 46 (1895): 198-205.

———. *The Theory of the Leisure Class*. 1899. New York: NAL, 1953.

Wiebe, Robert H. *The Search for Order: 1877-1920*. New York: Hill, 1967.

William, Kenny J. *In the City of Men: Another Story of Chicago*. Nashville: Townsend P, 1974.

Wilson, Edmund. "Henry Blake Fuller: The Art of Making It Flat." *New Yorker* 66 (1970): 112+.

Yeazell, Ruth Bernard. "The Conspicuous Wasting of Lily Bart." *ELH* 59 (1992): 713-34.

Ziff, Larzer. "Crushed Yet Complacent: Hamlin Garland and Henry Blake Fuller." *The American 1890's: Life and Times of a Lost Generation*. New York: Viking, 1968. 93-119.

Index

MODERN AMERICAN LITERATURE
New Approaches

Yoshinobu Hakutani, General Editor

The books in this series deal with many of the major writers known as American realists, modernists, and post-modernists from 1880 to the present. This category of writers will also include less known ethnic and minority writers, a majority of whom are African American, some are Native American, Mexican American, Japanese American, Chinese American, and others. The series might also include studies on well-known contemporary writers, such as James Dickey, Allen Ginsberg, Gary Snyder, John Barth, John Updike, and Joyce Carol Oates. In general, the series will reflect new critical approaches such as deconstructionism, new historicism, psychoanalytical criticism, gender criticism/ feminism, and cultural criticism.